"During my 30 years of helping people navigate the risks of public life, Eric Dezenhall has emerged as the most effective warrior and teacher. GLASS JAW offers the highest-resolution image of controversy in the new millennium, showing who wins, and how—who loses, and why."

—Gavin de Becker, author of the *New York Times*
bestseller, *The Gift of Fear*

"Today, one product defect, one offensive remark—combined with the power of instantaneous worldwide social networking—can bring down the mightiest giant. GLASS JAW analyzes how scandals spiral out of control and details the hard work required to regain a lost reputation. Dezenhall's cautionary tales are fascinating—and should serve as a stern warning to anyone with a reputation to lose."

—Daniel H. Pink, author of
To Sell Is Human and *Drive*

"I highly recommend Eric Dezenhall's GLASS JAW for anyone interested in reputational risk management in an age where no one is safe from scandal. GLASS JAW is like a wise cornerman teaching you how to take a public punch. No crisis is ever the same, but Dezenhall's book, rich with amusing examples and cautionary tales, will help you recognize if it's better to fight than to throw in the towel."

—Ian Bremmer, president, Eurasia Group, and
author of *Every Nation for Itself*

"With GLASS JAW, Eric Dezenhall once again offers fascinating and timely insights into the gladiatorial arena of modern crisis management. Like an Amazing Randi of communications, he debunks anyone claiming to perform PR magic as a fraud. Instead, he offers realistic strategies tempered by hard truths. We've been studying human behavior and how good and bad people react under great stress for quite some time, but we always learn something valuable from Eric.

—Former FBI Special Agent John Douglas and
Mark Olshaker, bestselling authors of *Mindhunter*,
The Anatomy of Motive, and *Law & Disorder*

"From Silicon Valley to the factories of the 'old' economy, marketplace power has never been more precarious. Eric Dezenhall's GLASS JAW is to damage control what Taleb's *Black Swan* is to economics— a jeremiad on how the seemingly powerful are increasingly at the mercy of the seemingly powerless. This book is the field guide anyone in a position of responsibility will want in the foxhole with them when their reputation is on the line."

—Deborah Perry Piscione, *New York Times*
bestselling author of *Secrets of Silicon Valley:*
What Everyone Else Can Learn from the
Innovation Capital of the World

GLASS JAW

A Manifesto for Defending Fragile
Reputations in an Age of Instant
Scandal

ERIC DEZENHALL

TWELVE

NEW YORK   BOSTON

Twelve
Hachette Book Group
1290 Avenue of the Americas
New York, NY 10104

www.HachetteBookGroup.com

Printed in the United States of America

RRD-C

First Edition: October 2014

10 9 8 7 6 5 4 3 2 1

Twelve is an imprint of Grand Central Publishing.
The Twelve name and logo are trademarks of Hachette Book Group, Inc.

The Hachette Speakers Bureau provides a wide range of authors for speaking events. To find out more, go to www.hachettespeakersbureau.com or call (866) 376-6591.

The publisher is not responsible for websites (or their content) that are not owned by the publisher.

Library of Congress Cataloging-in-Publication Data

Dezenhall, Eric.
    Glass jaw : a manifesto for defending fragile reputations in an age of instant scandal / Eric Dezenhall. — First edition.
        pages cm
    Includes index.
    ISBN 978-1-4555-8297-6 (hardback) — ISBN 978-1-4555-5800-1 (ebook) — ISBN 978-1-4789-8303-3 (audio download)   1. Public relations.
2. Reputation.   3. Public opinion.   4. Crisis management.
5. Corporate image.   I. Title.
    HD59.D487 2014
    659.2—dc23

                                                                    2014014006

To Ralph Ochsman (1920–2012)
Who survived Normandy and did all right for a poor kid from Philly

To Father Thomas L. Dixon (1934–2008)
Who understood the might of external forces

To Budd Schulberg (1914–2009)
Who knew a little about boxing and could write some, too

"Everybody's got plans . . . until they get hit."
—MIKE TYSON

Contents

SECTION III
The Physics of Controversy

SECTION IV
Redefining What It Means to Win

GLASS
JAW

HOW SCANDAL HAS CHANGED (AND HOW IT HASN'T)

1

The Fiasco Vortex

"Reality is that which, when you stop believing in it, doesn't go away."

—PHILIP K. DICK

In the mid-1970s, boxing fever had swept through the Philadelphia–South Jersey area, where I grew up. *Rocky*, which was famously set in Philadelphia, had just struck gold at the box office for Sylvester Stallone. Muhammad Ali lived in my hometown, Cherry Hill, New Jersey. Heavyweight champion Jersey Joe Walcott was a constant presence. Joe Frazier had long-standing ties to the region, as did Sonny Liston. Middleweight world champion Joey Giardello was a neighbor, and Mike "the Jewish Bomber" Rossman was making headlines.

Like a lot of teenage boys in the region, I had a brief delusion that I might be good at boxing. I accompanied a friend, Paul, who was a Golden Gloves champion, to the local Police Athletic League, a suburban boxing proving ground. I was relieved to see uniformed police officers there because without them the place would have looked like a Petri dish for the local rackets, which were at the height of their influence. I didn't feel especially safe.

Paul challenged me to pick out the best boxer in the place. My eyes soon fell upon a hulking man with thick muscles, black curly hair, and a little sunburn. He had just begun to dance around one of the rings with another boxer, who was smaller. The smaller man had brown, mousy hair. He wasn't skinny, but he didn't appear to have much muscle definition, either. He had pale skin, and looked as if he could be a stock boy at the hardware store down the street.

My prediction came easily: The Hulk was going to massacre the Stock Boy.

Paul nodded in ostensible agreement.

After what seemed to me like a lot of bouncing around, eventually the Hulk swung at the Stock Boy. I could hear the whooshing of his arm movements, but he hadn't connected with the Stock Boy, who wasn't doing anything impressive, just ducking away from the Hulk. I thought Paul had picked out a lousy fight for me to watch. I had been expecting Rocky versus Apollo. Cool moves. Mouthpieces flying out of the ring. This was about as third-rate an exhibition as I could imagine.

At about the same time that I lost my interest in the match, the Hulk went down. Hard. The punch the Stock Boy had thrown didn't seem particularly intense, but it worked.

Paul smirked and said, "Glass jaw." I didn't know what this term meant, but nodded because I didn't want to look like an idiot. I eventually gave Paul a quizzical look. "Glass jaw. A guy who can't take a punch," he said. "Usually a guy who looks like a badass."

Apparently, the Hulk was considered somewhat of a pathetic figure around this gym. A scary-looking guy who it would be unwise to tangle with in most circumstances, but who wasn't very gifted at what I was rapidly learning was a narrow discipline. The Stock Boy, on the other hand, who was nothing to look at, was well regarded in local boxing circles despite not having impressed me. Until he did.

The Hulk climbed out of the ring, dazed. I have a vague memory of hearing later about him having his jaw "wired shut" in order to heal. The concept of having wires in one's jaw was disturbing to me, but also exotic. It was one of those things that happened to a character in a Warner Bros. cartoon along with falling off cliffs or having anvils dropped on their heads.

I had been "training" on my own, which meant shadowboxing in front of my basement mirror, lifting weights, and hitting a make-shift heavy bag that I had crafted out of a duffel bag. I had grown impressed with my own abilities and had the kind of thought that teenagers with little life experience had: *Wait till the world gets a load of me.*

After the Hulk went down, I climbed into the ring with Paul. My next memory was of being on my back staring up at a skylight while Tweety Bird did the can-can around my head. Paul's concerned face hovered above me. He said, "You okay?"

Recognizing that I had failed to differentiate between sparring with a mirror, which didn't hit back, and fighting a Golden Gloves champion, who did, I ended my boxing career, 0-1.

My lesson of the day: *You never know who's a real tough guy until after the fight.*

I had assumed, based upon my general athleticism and untested performance, that I would either not get punched or be able to absorb one. It was the kind of foolishness one might expect from a teenager who had seen too much of one movie, but the lesson had been learned, and the term "glass jaw" has stingingly stuck with me: *"A guy who can't take a punch. Usually a guy who looks like a badass."*

I hadn't thought very much about the term "glass jaw" until about twenty years later. A client and friend named Harry, the communications troubleshooter at one of the largest chemical companies in the world, told me that he knew it was time to retire when his new boss alerted him to a chemical spill and said, "Get up here, Harry, we have a PR problem."

Harry's point was that when he was coming up in the business in the 1950s and 1960s, chemical spills were considered complex incidents of which the public relations function was just one component. You cleaned up the mess, compensated the community, alerted appropriate authorities, and put in new safeguards to prevent future such incidents. The curative process was long and painful, involving multiple disciplines, plenty of missteps, backtracking, and improvisation.

But make it *look good*? Or convince people not to be outraged? These were the things Harry's boss was now expecting of him.

In the 1990s, as cable news and the Internet were expanding, hostile coverage of corporate and political messes was becoming uncontrollable, but there was an expectation that the PR department could reach into a mythical bag of tricks and put a shine on a pigsty.

Harry shrugged and said, "Who the hell would believe that one of the biggest industrial companies on the planet couldn't take a punch?"

I didn't answer Harry's rhetorical question at the time, but will now: Like the Hulk whose downfall was so seared into my memory, powerful people and entities themselves are oblivious to the bogeys creeping around the ring and overestimate their skills to battle them. I have grown accustomed to the snickers of the unblemished who mistake their current fortunes for superior life management. The truth is that nobody who gets coldcocked believes they provoked or deserved it.

Glass Jaw *is about the changing nature of controversy. The thesis of this book is that individuals and organizations that were once thought to be indestructible are, in fact, uniquely fragile in the face of reputational attacks from conventionally weaker adversaries. David has become Goliath, and Goliath has become David. Today's attacks increasingly have life-of-their-own properties that fall beyond the reach of "management" in the sense of command-and-control direction. Some of this powerlessness is due to a basic diagnostic error: The tendency to address reputational crises as if they are "communications problems" versus something larger and more structural, not to mention aggravated by the viral pathology of the controversy surrounding them. In fact, the image-making industry that purports to have cures to reputational attacks is every bit the paper tiger as those it claims to be helping, and it richly deserves demystification.*

The glass jaw concept—the idea that the powerful are brittle under certain conditions—begins with a common misjudgment. Just as I had based my incorrect assessment of a boxer's ability on a cognitive bias that mistook the *appearance* of fighting ability for actual skill, Harry's boss was abetting failure by conflating a complex event, a chemical spill, with one that could be materially affected by PR tactics. Part and parcel of this misdiagnosis was the false expectation that there was something to "win" for Harry's company when the real objective was to cut their losses, an unattractive pitch you'll never hear from an ad agency.

Harry's boss incorrectly estimated the level of control the company had over public opinion, perhaps believing that someone of Harry's talents and connections could "spin" things with the same ease and authority that one might phone in a pizza order.

The media landscape is littered with an expanding universe of glass-jawed protagonists. Down the rabbit hole of scandal, the weak are strong, the strong are weak, and this Wonderland is populated by odd and fierce characters and unpredictable vectors.

One of the better artistic renderings of this dimensional change occurred in the HBO film *Phil Spector*, about the legendary record producer who was convicted of murdering down-on-her-luck actress Lana Clarkson. Al Pacino, portraying a fictionalized Spector, shows up to his murder trial in a huge blond fright wig. On the eve of trial, "Spector" lashes out during a court preparatory session, admonishing his legal team about who he is and, more important, who his accusers are—nobodies. "Spector's" lawyer, played by

Helen Mirren, wisely decides not to let him testify, and when "Spector" shows up at court in the fright wig, she becomes physically ill. To "Spector," he is Zeus, but to the court, as the judge's expression betrays, he's just a murderous little freak.

The real Spector is now in prison, most likely for the rest of his life. His fright wig serves as a symbol of the inability of once-mighty figures to transition between dimensions of scandal, largely because they can fathom neither how they are perceived nor how much power they have lost to the ghosts hidden within the scandal machine.

Other scandals with glass-jawed principals:

- Toyota, which endured multiple recalls involving nine million cars in 2009–2011 after allegations that its vehicles spontaneously accelerated due to an engine defect, despite the eventual disproving of this theory;
- The once-unassailable Susan G. Komen for the Cure breast cancer foundation, which was battered after announcing it would cease funding breast examinations at Planned Parenthood facilities;
- "Lean finely textured beef," labeled "pink slime," a popular form of processed meat that was wrongly characterized as being an unsafe additive, which devastated sectors of the meat industry;
- lululemon, the fast-rising yoga gear manufacturer and retailer that took a hit when its flagship brand of yoga pants was recalled due to an extremely visible defect;
- Paula Deen, the southern-style chef who was pilloried in the media and lost lucrative business partnerships with the likes of Wal-Mart and the Food Network when she admitted in a lawsuit deposition to having used a racial epithet in the distant past;

- A&E *Duck Dynasty* television series patriarch Phil Robertson, who imperiled his hit show when his remarks about how the Bible views homosexuality were published in an interview in *GQ* magazine;
- Golf superstar Tiger Woods, who lost his marriage, several endorsements, and an estimated $50 million in annual income after a 2009 car crash that unleashed secrets about his private life, which stood in sharp contrast to his above-reproach reputation. Investors in the companies that endorsed Tiger endured a paper loss of $5–12 billion in the weeks following the crash;
- Penn State and Joe Paterno: The arrest of child molester and former defensive Coach Jerry Sandusky crippled the university's storied football program and the reputation of Paterno, the coach who built it;
- General Stanley McChrystal, who was deposed from his command in Afghanistan for making critical comments about Obama administration leadership, even though there was a big difference between what McChrystal actually said and what he was perceived to have said;
- BP's catastrophic oil spill in 2010, which dumped 4.9 million barrels of oil into the Gulf of Mexico, did tens of billions of dollars in damage to the regional economy and habitat, and cost the company $25 billion to clean up the spill and help regenerate the economy;
- Mitt Romney, whose 2012 presidential campaign was derailed by a video taken by a bartender working at a fund-raising event, which showed Romney characterizing 47 percent of Americans as unwilling to take responsibility for their own affairs, instead relying on government support;
- The Duke University lacrosse players who, in 2006, were falsely accused of rape and were widely characterized by mainstream media as being guilty;

- Martha Stewart, who was convicted of lying to the authorities in conjunction with allegations of insider trading in pharmaceutical stock, ImClone. She went to prison;
- Movie distributor Netflix, which announced plans to alter its pricing structure—effectively a price hike—and spin off its DVD service, invited such consumer outrage that the company reversed its policy soon after announcing the change;
- News Corporation, which endured a scandal surrounding illegal telephone hacking and bribery, leading to criminal prosecutions, top-management casualties, and a loss of $7 billion in market capitalization over a four-day period in 2011;
- Carnival Cruise Lines, which faced both the capsizing of one ship (belonging to a subsidiary), the *Costa Concordia*, killing thirty-two people, and mechanical failures on the *Carnival Triumph* that left thousands of passengers stranded on a ship filled with human waste;
- The reputation of Livestrong, the charity established by cycling champion Lance Armstrong to raise awareness and research funding for cancer, a disease that he survived, was rocked when Armstrong finally admitted to serial use of performance-enhancing drugs;
- Entertainer Michael Jackson, who was accused and eventually acquitted of child molestation charges despite withering coverage of his travails;
- Manti Te'o, the Notre Dame linebacker whose beloved girlfriend died of leukemia. It turned out that she did not exist;
- Anthony Weiner, whose predilection for oversharing his nether regions online led to twin downfalls: the end of his congressional career and his campaign for mayor of New York City;

- New Jersey governor Chris Christie, whose presidential trajectory was knocked off course by charges that he deliberately ordered a traffic jam to avenge a local mayor who didn't support him in his recent race;
- Consumer products and drug giant Johnson & Johnson, celebrated for decades as the gold standard of crisis management, was rocked by dozens of back-to-back recalls and a management shakeup tied largely to product safety and quality allegations; and
- The National Security Agency and defense contractor Booz Allen, which were turned upside down in the spring of 2013 when contractor Edward Snowden leaked government secrets to the *Guardian* newspaper and touched off an unwanted debate about invasive government spying.

What *Glass Jaw* lacks in magic tricks to make events such as these vanish, it will seek to make up for in no-nonsense insight into minimizing the chances of becoming ensnared in controversy and negotiating it if you must. Think of it this way: If you find yourself in a foxhole surrounded by shelling, it may be of some comfort to have the field notes of someone who has been in one before.

None of Us Is Immune

Nor are the mighty the only examples of glass-jawed targets. The news is replete with examples of everyday people who, due to foolishness or bad luck, find themselves on the receiving end of disproportionate humiliation. From the cavalcade of folks who implicate themselves in crimes on social media to the victims of bad breakups who find salacious rumors and photos of themselves on the Internet, to innocent bystanders who have been identified by major news outlets as murderers, few of us are exempt from getting ensnared under the wrong collision of circumstances.

Have none of us ever made a snide remark about an acquaintance, written an email on a sensitive subject, forwarded an ignorant joke, made a flirty comment, done something stupid in college, been in a situation where we'd rather not be photographed, opened a raunchy or peculiar Internet link, made a poor decision that we'd rather not have memorialized, or made an enemy who remains motivated to hurt us? (If not, you are surely a special individual.) Prior to current media conditions, we sinners could deny things, discreetly repent, or move on and reinvent ourselves. Today, the worst aspects of ourselves are suspended in digital museums for the world to behold and recoil from forever.

Despite the sheer number of messes like those highlighted in this book, the fallacies surrounding the origins and nature of controversy are getting further and further off the mark. When Lance Armstrong's career imploded in late 2012, I received countless calls from reporters, virtually all of them asking me why Armstrong was botching his *handling* of the mess. I declined to provide commentary because I knew some of the players on Armstrong's team and respected them. I had no intention of joining the Greek chorus of pundits whose main qualification for declaring Armstrong's crisis to have been mismanaged was their willingness to go on TV and say so. I had worked on athlete doping cases before and knew that vindication was very, very rare. And I couldn't believe that otherwise sophisticated reporters thought the key issue in Armstrong's implosion was the inability of his team to stop the hemorrhage of terrible media coverage and litigation, as opposed to his original sins: the decades-long doping and cheating conspiracy.

My point in *Glass Jaw* should not be misconstrued to mean that giant corporations and influential people will no longer have power. Of course they will; oil companies will continue to drill for fossil fuel and computer companies will develop faster microprocessors; nongovernmental organizations (NGOs) will continue to ameliorate hunger and promote conservation; and celebrities will continue to appear on magazine covers and walk down red carpets. *However, when it comes to the narrow pathology of reputational and marketplace attacks, these behemoths are shockingly vulnerable to agenda-driven and organic disruptions beyond their control. At the same time, those who were once thought powerless—individual consumers, issue-driven activists— have become more powerful than ever and sometimes even qualify as conventional powers in and of themselves.*

The word "reputation" carries with it a whiff of narcissism, as if concern about one's reputation is a vanity that exists separate from the practicalities of everyday living. However, this book views reputational damage as an extremely tangible phenomenon that ruins lives, careers, and businesses, which are the concerns of my professional life.

Motiveless Malignancy

This book seeks to define the new reality, one where "little guys" can injure "big guys" who don't have the will to fight little guys and don't even have the tools to do it. I think of the scene in *Raiders of the Lost Ark* where Indiana Jones (Harrison Ford) encounters a fearsome Arab warrior who elaborately demonstrates his lethal capabilities with a sword and a sinister laugh so that Indiana knows the horrible fate that awaits him. With an expression of minor annoyance, Indiana simply grabs his handgun out of his holster and shoots the warrior dead. It never occurred to the swordsman that neither his immense size nor his swordsmanship were relevant when facing a smaller man with a revolver.

Attacks on conventional powers by "irregular" or "guerrilla" (literal translation "small war") forces are not new. What is new is the growing number and intensity of asymmetric forces *combined with* the powerful weapons now available to them: porous and incriminating communications devices like email and thumb drives, uncontrollable Internet communications and social media, and a geometrically expanding "mainstream" media universe that is catalyzed by damaging information—true or false—and hostile to nuance and context. We live in a period of chain reactions, which render many controversies self-compounding.

One element of this overdetermination is scandal coverage itself, which triggers a comparatively new, self-invented pundit class that declares the controversy to have been mismanaged, which, in turn, ignites multiple *additional* rounds of coverage, causing the vortex to spin even faster to its inevitable conclusion.

I don't believe that the nature of scandal has changed because human nature is not any different from how it used to be. What's new is the *conductivity* of controversy. Multiplying media, the unfettered access to "weapons of the weak" such as the Internet, the industrialization of leaking, combined with the sheer speed and reach of these conduits, have allowed the conventionally weak to injure their targets with devastating efficiency. In the past, "long-form" journalism that examined issues in depth could alter the momentum of a chain reaction, but such journalism for larger audiences is by and large dead.

It may seem like the present ecosystem is conspiring against us, but I think of the conductivity of the digital frontier as having a "motiveless malignancy," a term the poet Coleridge used to describe *Othello*'s Iago: It is not inherently agenda-driven, but its power strongly suggests a will to destruction.

I see no evidence that consumers of scandal care if the information they receive is accurate. There is very little outrage or sense of betrayal when information turns out to be wrong, as long as it resonates. In a story about political scandals, the *Washington Post*'s Paul

Farhi concluded, "By the time a more conclusive picture of guilt or innocence emerges . . . the coverage has often moved on, leaving the original impression largely unrebutted."

There is an addictive quality to the consumption of controversy as there is with other addictive activities such as overeating. Do we overeat because we truly need more sustenance or because we are driven by the habit of sticking something in our mouths regardless of its nutritional value? Processing negative narratives isn't about enlightenment, it's about stimuli.

I think of what's happening now as the "Fiasco Vortex" in the sense of snowball effects, vicious circles, and feedback loops that magnify destructive information and spread beyond the reach of available treatments. The Fiasco Vortex is one part crisis and three parts farce, the farce encircling the crisis and whipping it into an exponentially destructive beast beyond mitigation. Wrote Matthew DeBord in a *Washington Post* piece appropriately titled "The Crisis in Crisis PR," "The lesson for companies that screw up is that you really have no chance: The currents are against you from the get-go. The courts of Twitter and online video sharing and the forming of Facebook groups to deplore the transgressions of an enterprise will overwhelm even the most crafted crisis battle plan. The profession, quite simply, is at a crossroads. And it isn't in a position to ride out the bumps, because it's up against the kind of high-altitude turbulence that can shred the airframe."

Major businesses and institutions are gradually beginning to recognize that the basic physics of communication have shifted. A new study by Deloitte concluded that reputational damage represents the top strategic risk facing corporations. A Deloitte executive summarized: "The time it takes for damaging news to spread is quicker, it goes to a wider audience more easily, and the record of it is stored digitally for longer." As we will see, factors including denial, fear of career obsolescence, and false hope in volatile and unproven techniques like social media define the prevailing mentality in many big outfits.

Lighting a Forest Fire Versus Putting One Out

Glass Jaw is also an indictment of a flawed belief system, of category error. The misguided building blocks of this belief system are that:

1. The original sin or adverse event is somehow collateral to the fallout of that sin or event, as opposed to being its true catalyst. In other words, the idea that the scandal spun out of control primarily because of its *handling*;
2. The scandal protagonist or "principal" can control the controversy's outcome and the antagonists who are actively fueling it, especially with the help of an all-powerful image-making industry;
3. The resolution lies in adherence to public relations scripture— if the protagonist had simply implemented the accepted curative actions (that he or she failed to implement for some reason) then the situation would have been resolved and the negative perception dislodged from memory; and
4. There are "solutions," as we understand them to be, at all.

This is a "facts-of-life" book about the capricious and metastatic nature of modern controversy and scandal where the "facts" are based in my decades of experiences in the war rooms of crisis management. It is a memoir of insight versus autobiography and contains the kinds of observations I share with clients and students. I am hired by those who are anticipating or embroiled in controversy, who are enduring intense criticism—corporations, public institutions, prominent individuals—and they want me to shepherd them through the storm so they can return to their pre-scandal lives.

Throughout the book, I will make observations that I hope will have practical utility. I am, however, reluctant to characterize this as an advice book because I believe that cookie-cutter counsel about crisis management is what's wrong with the entire enterprise. Rather, I am seeking to offer wisdom through the deconstruction of complex phenomena. The development of cures begins with getting the diagnosis right rather than promoting superficial salves and palliatives.

In this spirit, more than one person has suggested to me that Bill Clinton should write a crisis management book. I disagree. Clinton, a preternatural crisis manager, would have no formula to add any more than actress Scarlett Johansson could teach us anything about being sexy. Clinton's crisis management strategy is *being* Bill Clinton. Scarlett's attractiveness "strategy" is that she's Scarlett Johansson. Their attributes are not replicable or scalable. As Johansson's character, Nola, in the film *Match Point*, said about the tendency for men to become obsessed with her, "Men always seem to wonder. They think I'd be something very special."

Indeed, some people and organizations *are* special, as are the conditions that contribute the controversies that make or break them. Universal principles are the scourge of damage control. It is a lot more comforting to believe all of us have the charisma to be Clinton or Johansson than it is to accept the harshness of real-world inequality and powerlessness.

To these stark ends, I will define the new realities of damage control. Exclamations by the besieged such as, "We have to push back!" beg the question, "With what?" "Pushing back" requires weapons and constituents: Targets of attack often don't *have* either. You can't beat something with nothing.

Why would the smartest, most powerful people and entities the world has ever known consistently fail to get themselves out of reputational disasters? Because the solutions are never easy. How could Rupert Murdoch's News Corporation, which critics view as the very symbol of corporate hegemony and mass manipulation, fail to extricate itself from its bribery and phone hacking scandal? The debacle cost Murdoch the jobs of his protégé, Rebekah Brooks, and his son James, not to mention the loss of billions in shareholder value and hundreds of millions in legal fees, penalties, and settlements.

The short answer is that it's a lot easier to light a forest fire than it is to put one out. Even when a firefighting effort succeeds, what remains is a big mess. In fact, the realistic objective of crisis management is to endure controversy, not escape it.

The new crisis management road map is that there is no road map because there is no road, at least not yet. The road is still being built, destroyed, and rebuilt every minute, and the operating climate leaves targets of attack with less power to combat the forces lined up against it. What works for one party in one set of circumstances will not work for another party facing different conditions. Crisis management is an improvisational art, not a laboratory science. And sometimes the improvisation works; other times it doesn't.

When I have spoken about the glass jaw phenomenon, more than a few friends (and critics) have said, "So what?" *Attacks on the mighty have got to be good things. If a few conglomerates or big shots go down, well, perhaps in the scheme of things, it will be a warning to others to curb their dark impulses.*

It's hard to argue with this position because you can't change a belief system embraced by a large swath of the population. It's especially challenging when so many examples of genuine malfeasance litter the landscape. The torrent of corporate crime and the incarceration of top executives are unprecedented, and it's safe to assume that a lot of them are guilty. Attacks on powerful targets come in varying degrees of legitimacy. I don't believe that all attacks are unjustified fabrications, and there is plenty of good scholarship to prove this point.

During the course of my career, I have become increasingly disillusioned with much corporate behavior, not because I have witnessed many diabolical acts—they happen less than you think—but because the sheer size, lack of commitment, and drive to make money have rendered many businesses oblivious to their customers, employees, communities, and shareholders. The very same glass jaw phenomenon that I am analyzing here is one that can some-times be an effective check on the lack of humanity that defines our interactions with our institutions. In fact, I have enjoyed helping "little guy" clients find and amplify their voices because I believed their criticism of "Goliaths" *was* justified.

As targets have become more vulnerable and the devices to repair the damage have grown more elusive, the spin industry, para-doxically, has enjoyed unprecedented mythologizing far beyond what it can actually deliver. The outrageous portrayals and percep-tions of public relations people, which we will explore, reveal an unintended truth: The gut-level belief that targets are guilty and deserving of ruin is validated by the fallacy that their handlers must be deploying dark arts to vindicate them.

In a waiting room prior to a TV interview about celebrity chef Paula Deen's scandal, a reporter with whom I would be sparring commented about how Deen had botched her crisis management. I asked him to tell me specifically what she had done wrong once her deposition went public.

He said, "She should have immediately gotten Oprah Winfrey, Jesse Jackson, and Al Sharpton to get behind her."

"On what planet could that have been arranged at all, let alone *immediately*?" I asked, then added: "There are two impossible errands: Getting people to like an oil company and convincing people you're not a racist."

He muttered something again about her having "botched" it, and that was that.

While we will examine Deen's situation more closely, the reality is that only in Hollywood portrayals of scandal management could the Oprah-Jesse-Al trifecta been scored immediately, if at all. But this utterly delusional expectation was conveyed both on and off the air as a statement of fact. Damage control is sorcery provided you don't actually have to do it, and the thinking around it bounces between the utopian and the hackneyed.

Writing and Reading *Glass Jaw*

I will make observations and generalizations in this book, and I will draw conclusions based on lessons learned during my career. Academic studies are everywhere, but experience is precious. My data are the dividends of hard-won experience, including wins and losses, and the changes in the culture and tools we use.

I have seen scandal figures be right and win, be right and lose, be wrong and win, and be wrong and lose. This wisdom has been sufficiently persuasive to me that I regard what I have learned as vital operating intelligence. As defense attorney William Taylor has said, "The value of experience is learning to see how things are going to turn out when they begin."

I have biases, and they favor the targets of attack, even if those targets are big companies that aren't very cuddly. I am constantly reevaluating my worldview, questioning prevailing dogma, considering new variables in the operating climate, and discarding tactics I once thought were brilliant but no longer work in the new environment.

Given client confidences, I cannot betray many of the specific experiences that brought about these lessons, but I will share key takeaways. I will sometimes use composite examples or otherwise obscure the identities of the players. In some cases, I will recall things that happened a long time ago and have done my best to reflect them as accurately as possible.

I am skeptical of most crisis management case studies because I find much of what scandal principals are being advised, and what is being taught in business and management classes, to be corrupted by self-serving conclusions and deep ideological and methodological biases. Advice only has value if it has been tested and shown to work with relative consistency. Counsel rooted in how we wish the world worked isn't counsel at all; it's just dogma.

Furthermore, those who have escaped or mitigated crises don't want to poke around old dynamite by congratulating themselves in case studies on the cataclysm that never happened. Most of those who have survived scandal simply want to get on with their lives, not leave a record of the most miserable episode of their existences. Accordingly, some of the best case studies have never and will never be written or published.

I will use the terms "crisis," "controversy," and "scandal" somewhat interchangeably. For our purposes, let's keep it simple and use the terms to mean an unwanted event or circumstance that causes reputational and other practical damage to an individual or organization. Think oil spills, product defects and recalls, criminal allegations, financial fraud, offensive statements or policies, sexual indiscretions, competitive assaults, "lawfare" (warfare through harassing litigation), and brand damage.

While the challenges associated with managing crises for businesses, other large institutions, and individuals differ, I am accustomed to referring to business organizations, which is why references to companies will predominate. Other times, I will use the term "principal" to describe the protagonist of a controversy, which encompasses both organizations and individuals.

> **Takeaway:** In the course of the thirty years I have been in the crisis management trade, controversies have become more lethal and more damaging to people and institutions. Central to this lethality is the same kind of self-delusion about one's strengths that afflicted the big boxer in my hometown. The antiquated and charlatanic lessons being taught about how to navigate dynamic and high-stakes situations need either rehabilitation or to be put out to pasture. This book dissects the new physics of our operating climate.

2

When Scandal Went
to Sleep

"It'll get worse now because it'll go faster."
—FINANCIER JULES STEINHARDT, *WALL STREET 2*
(AS PORTRAYED BY ELI WALLACH)

One of my first experiences in the field of high-stakes communications was as a young aide in the White House Office of Communications during the Reagan administration. This was the early 1980s, and the media environment, which we thought was adversarial at the time, was, in contrast to today, rather cordial.

The author of President Reagan's media strategy was Michael K. Deaver. He was the first person to whom I heard the term "spin doctor" applied. I remember when I heard Mike described this way, too, as he was also regarded as Reagan's "image maker." This timing teaches an important lesson.

In August and September 1982, the economy was in a terrible state. "Reaganomics Sucks" was spray-painted on buildings, bridges, and benches around Washington. Conventional wisdom was that Virginia governor Chuck Robb was a shoo-in for the White House in 1984. There was chatter about impeachment and rumors that

Reagan's top staff would be replaced. This was frightening to me because even though I was at the bottom of the food chain, I was thrilled to be in the White House and envisioned a career in politics: If the guys at the top were vulnerable—Chief of Staff James A. Baker III, Counselor Edwin Meese, and Deputy Chief of Staff Mike Deaver—then what would happen to kids like me?

I need not have worried.

In October, the conventional wisdom swung wildly in the opposite direction. Reagan's staffers were hailed as geniuses. Glowing profiles were soon written about them.

What happened?

The stock market rallied, and a wave of euphoria infected the republic. The few pundits who existed in that era began referring to Deaver as a "spin doctor," a mystical healer of reputations. I marveled over this sea change to Deaver himself, and he responded with a shrug and said something that he was to repeat often about the service he provided to Reagan: "I just lit him well." Meaning that he hadn't created Reagan's image; he just helped exploit his natural strengths.

The subtext of Mike's message was that the White House staff hadn't done anything miraculous to alter Reagan's image in the fall of 1982; the economy had simply pulled out of recession, and the reactive cultural noise attributed this to genius.

Mike Deaver's modesty aside—he was a brilliant man—there was nothing mysterious about what he did. He placed Reagan in situations where he was naturally strong and avoided putting him where he was weak. "Almost everything we do is determined by whether we think it will get on the network news shows in the evening," White House spokesman Larry Speakes told the Associated Press. Time and space were precious, and it wasn't a herculean task to get the leader of the free world placed on the three evening network news programs. Whether that news would be favorable was a different matter.

The Reagan White House established a "line-of-the-day" message management strategy whereby the administration emphasized one major theme with the media per day. This theme was likely to be reported because, in addition to the three evening news shows, the line of the day was primarily targeted against three national newspapers, the *Washington Post, New York Times,* and *Wall Street Journal,* from which much broadcast news derived.*

The highly focused line-of-the-day strategy wouldn't work in today's climate, where the standard has become the "bite of the nanosecond." In the 1980s, the three evening newscasts reached 55 million Americans who couldn't talk back to their screens. Presidential administrations and other powerful organizations try for message discipline and occasionally succeed, but with hundreds of prominent media outlets, millions of blogs, and billions of social media exchanges every day, any suggestion of control is a fantasy.

More media means less nuance. "Long-form journalism" is dying because the marketplace wants quick bursts of information that titillate and confirm existing prejudices. In the fight for public opinion, the better story wins, and in the Fiasco Vortex, it's all about the story—sentiments, not thoughts. Feeling is achieved via signs, not data. Think about the trinity of corporate scandal visuals that accompanies most coverage: the aerial photo of the villain's mansion, the photo of the villain's much younger and entitled-looking second or third wife, and the photo of the rightly despairing pensioners who have lost their retirement funds. *This*—Hannibal Lecter, Cruella de Vil, and the Haunted Mansion—are shorthand for a witch hunt, never mind the context and complex dynamics of what caused the collapse.

---

* *USA Today* had just launched and had not yet become a big focus of media relations.

Stories should not be mistaken for lies; they are poetic truths. There is a basis in reality even if that reality isn't the antidote it claims to be. Barack Obama's rise was memorialized quite literally in a sign: Shepard Fairey's iconic, red, white, and blue poster featuring Obama's image and the words "HOPE" and "CHANGE." Whether you supported Obama or did not, these images were not false. They were sentimental encapsulations of what many people felt, namely, that a smart, young, exciting, attractive, biracial leader could deliver us from the stale muck of two wars and a collapsed economy.

Sentiments cannot be proven or disproven, only felt in the context of the players and the times. Obama, who authored two autobiographies by early middle age, knew there was fuel in his story, and he ran it right into the White House despite the failed attempts of his detractors to characterize it as a lie. Obama's personal history, when combined with contextual variables, was simply a better story than the false notion that he was a foreign-born Muslim.

The Ascendance of Velocity

There are few better stories than a scandal, but scandal demands emotional resonance in order to launch. When it comes to receiving information, consumers find accuracy to be a helpful seasoning but are more concerned with the salivating effect of having been served a salty snack. Scandal memes are like potato chips, delicious in a short-term way but not good for you. *So what, keep 'em coming.*

If the Vietnam War and Watergate scandal were the main accelerants of perpetual controversy in the late 1960s and 1970s, the emergence of ABC's *Nightline* certified its permanence. Created as *America Held Hostage* to temporarily cover the capture of American hostages in Iran, *Nightline* became a staple of high-octane news coverage that remains on television more than thirty years later.

Coverage of controversy graduated from its embryonic to fetal stages with the 1991 Persian Gulf War, when CNN's broadcast of the conflict forced millions of Americans accustomed to network news to explore cable. The intersection of cable's organic expansion and the Monica Lewinsky scandal in the late 1990s catalyzed shows like MSNBC's *Hardball* and Fox News, which hit Clinton harder than most media. In addition, news aggregator the *Drudge Report* and other online outlets grew out of this.

The amplification of conflict was—and remains—the fuel for these developments. Put differently, all parties involved gain from the perpetuation of hostilities, and consumers of news are not innocent bystanders: We love it. A colleague at my firm who covered the Clinton-Lewinsky scandal at a major television news organization laughed as he recalled man-on-the-street interviews where subjects claimed to be "sick of hearing about the president's sex life." Said my colleague, "Every time we changed the subject away from Clinton and Lewinsky, we could see the ratings drop off the cliff." So they went back to covering the president's sex life.*

Among other consequences, the velocity of news has led to the tyranny of speed over accuracy. Where journalistic mistakes were once professional crimes, today they are misdemeanors, if that.

The Associated Press and *Boston Globe* inaccurately reported that arrests had been made in the April 2013 Boston Marathon bombings when they had not. CNN had reported that suspects had been identified before they had been. The social media site Reddit incorrectly identified the bombing suspects and published photos of innocent people online and soon apologized. Several online and mainstream media sites incorrectly identified a missing Brown University student, Sunil Tripathi, as one of the bombers. The troubled Tripathi was found dead—having nothing to do with the false reports, but

---

* It was in the spirit of "sex sells" and "if it bleeds it leads" that *Rolling Stone* put accused Boston bomber Dzokhar Tsarnaev (looking like a rock star) on its cover. Sales jumped 102 percent.

the damage to his and his family's reputation had been done. The *New York Post* identified two young men as bombing suspects on its front page along with their photographs and the headline "BAG MEN," a reference to the backpacks the real bombers carried. The men have sued the *Post* for defamation.

In the hours following the September 2013 mass shootings at the Washington, D.C., Navy Yard, numerous media outlets reported that the killer had used an AR-15 automatic rifle, the type that had been used in other recent tragedies, and instinctively characterized it as an "assault rifle." The *New York Daily News'* headline read, "Same Gun Different Slay." Other outlets reporting the AR-15 angle included the *Washington Post, New York Times, Los Angeles Times, USA Today*, MSNBC, CNN, and *Buzzfeed*. The FBI denied that there was any evidence that such a weapon had been used. Rather, the shooter had used a shotgun and handgun.

Even worse, a man named Rollie Chance was falsely identified as the Navy Yard killer on CBS Radio (later corrected) and on tweets from NBC and CBS reporters. Similarly, multiple media identified the *brother* of Newtown, Connecticut, killer Adam Lanza as the mass murderer after the December 2012 horror.

In May 2007, a false report on a technology blog about a delayed iPhone release lopped $4 billion off Apple's market capitalization. In October 2008, Apple stock lost 10 percent of its value when a false rumor bounced across the Web that CEO Steve Jobs had suffered a heart attack.

Among the factors contributing to the velocity of news is the shift in the role of the public from being consumers of news, as we were during Watergate, to participants and antagonists. Many of the tips that have led to both inaccurate news reports and, paradoxically, corrective measures have come from citizen journalists and tipsters.

As the Fiasco Vortex has grown ever more savage, those who expect themselves to become targets have become better prepared for counterattack. When Dan Rather ran an erroneous news report on *60 Minutes* suggesting that George W. Bush had avoided military service in Vietnam and had shirked his duties in the Texas Air National Guard, it was little-known blogs that kept the mighty CBS in check. Rather was notorious in Republican circles for his adversarial relationship with party leaders going back to Richard Nixon, and the Bush family specifically. When the story about Bush ran, the conservative-leaning blogs Little Green Footballs, Power Line, Allahpundit, and Free Republic entered the controversy by mobilizing forensic experts that showed why the Rather documents were frauds. Legacy media outlets such as the *Washington Post* and *USA Today* joined the examination and began airing reports that reached similar conclusions to what the blogs were suggesting.

After repeatedly standing by its coverage and after an internal investigation, CBS admitted that it should not have used the documents. Several *60 Minutes* officials were terminated, and Dan Rather himself retired in 2005. His retirement was never directly linked to the *60 Minutes* report on Bush, but such associations are rarely made publicly.

In echoes of the Rather debacle, in November 2013, CBS *60 Minutes* apologized for a story about the Benghazi, Libya, attack in September 2012 that claimed the lives of Ambassador Christopher Smith and three others. In its urgency to air the story, *60 Minutes* had used a former security officer as a source who claimed he had been present during the attacks but had told the FBI that he had not.

Journalistic debacles have happened for a long time, but the velocity of information has caused news organizations that should know better to take risks that they shouldn't. Even if bad coverage falls short of libel, it can cause terrible damage. It's a lot easier to create a mess in the Fiasco Vortex than to clean one up. Today, if you're talking about a scandal, you're, well, still talking about it, stirring it up in the public consciousness.

In the past, there were physical barriers to stirring things up: finite media with firm deadlines, limited access, and almost no validating surveillance (in the form of cell phone photos, documents leaked in real time, 24/7 pundits, and blogs). We went from an evening news cycle in the 1980s to an hourly news cycle in the 1990s to a real-time Twitter cycle in the late 2000s. In fact, the Twitter cycle isn't really a cycle at all, just an endless rapid-fire series of data bursts.

Some of my students, who are younger than the Internet, were surprised to learn that in the not-too-distant past, there was a certain time of night when television broadcasting just stopped; all that remained on the screen was the image of a billowing American flag or the test pattern.

Like everything else, scandal went to sleep.

The Omen: A Car Possessed

My first hint that something was changing in the crisis management dynamic occurred in the mid-1980s. I was working for a large international public relations firm that was handling the Audi account when *60 Minutes* ran its seminal story alleging that the Audi 5000 engaged in "sudden acceleration." This led to an avalanche of stories, largely driven by plaintiffs' attorneys representing members of the "Audi Victims Network"—Audi 5000 owners who claimed that their cars rocketed out of control without any apparent action on the part of the driver. Many of these stories appeared on regional market TV stations where drivers in the region, taking their cues from the national *60 Minutes* broadcast, gave their localized versions of sudden acceleration.

Audi dispatched its executives along with media specialists like myself to these local markets to deal with the adversarial coverage. It quickly became clear that nothing we did to demonstrate the scientific impossibility of sudden acceleration defused the hysteria. The main problem was that Audi executives ended up "debating" with distressed "Audi victims." In a fight between a nice person—the people who claimed to have experienced sudden acceleration—and an executive from a big auto company (which happened to be . . . German), the nice person with the tears in her eyes wins.

Here we were, the well-compensated wizards with all of the science and the resources and skills to impart that science, and nothing we were doing was stopping the onslaught against the Audi 5000. To the extent we were making a mistake, it was one of strategic misassumption, as opposed to tactical failure: This fight had nothing to do with science. It was being fought out on an entirely different frequency. That frequency was the one that transmits emotion, blame, anger, ratings, and money, not "the facts" that had been so carefully packaged in press kits. In a battle between science and spectacle, spectacle wins.

As bad as this experience was, there was one thing we were able to do in those days that we couldn't do today. We could go to sleep for a few hours and regroup in the morning because there was a point when the media, and the people driving the attack on the Audi 5000, also went to sleep. Nonetheless, it took almost two decades for Audi to recover.

The 1990s marked a turning point for the conventional power of corporations to defuse attacks. One factor was the tabloidization of network attack programs such as *Dateline NBC*, *Primetime Live*, *60 Minutes*, and *48 Hours*, which reached their heights in audience and respectability. It was hard to fight these programs, which were being constantly fed packaged stories by plaintiffs' lawyers equipped with victims, villains, and vindicators. The victims are the vulnerable players injured by the villains, the main targets of the investigation. Bringing these misdeeds to light are the vindicators, the impartial authorities such as reporters or watchdogs.

Vindicator

Villain

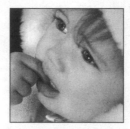

Victim

Contrary to the popular notion that big companies hold their advertising dollars over the heads of network executives like the Sword of Damocles, this is rarely practiced. Why not? Companies are afraid that their heavy-handedness will detonate even greater controversy. Besides, they need the visibility that advertising brings.

As with all uncontested powers, however, some of these outlets got sloppy. In 1993, *Dateline NBC* rigged a General Motors pickup truck to explode in order to demonstrate its flammability. This was a watershed moment in damage control. For one thing, General Motors fought back and forced an apology from NBC, which also fired several reporters.* For another, it showed corporations that the news media were not incorruptible jurists but for-profit enterprises

---

* It's worth noting that *Dateline*'s ratings were significantly higher in the summer *after* the GM imbroglio.

that had strong incentives to injure unlovable targets, independent of the truth.

The period roughly between the *Dateline* affair in 1993 and the full emergence of the Internet in the late 1990s was the heyday of crisis management. Companies were emboldened to fight back, there were straightforward countermeasures—advertising, media relations, media appearances, lobbying—and motivated adversaries hadn't yet figured out how to fully leverage the Internet as a weapon.

Throughout this heyday, the mythical 1982 Tylenol tampering* crisis management "case study" was being appropriated by publicity firms as evidence of *their* capabilities, and hysterical companies that had just received inquiries from *60 Minutes* were all too happy to be persuaded that they had found their Madison Avenue fixer.

In the 1990s, the media were desperate for tabloid-style ratings; a new generation of media, not steeped in the journalistic traditions of rigor, was recklessly taking over. Plaintiffs' lawyers, emboldened by tobacco industry lawsuit settlements in the hundreds of billions, were at the height of their influence. Upon joining my firm, a former producer of a network magazine show claimed that she got more than three-quarters of her stories from plaintiffs' lawyers.

Moreover, the pandemic of damning emails that defines our age had not yet metastasized—there actually had to *be* a discovery process before such things surfaced. Finally, corporate innovators had a swashbuckling vibe prior to the scandals of the early 2000s; they were more willing to hit back, and their adversaries had not yet defined the dodgy shibboleths (e.g., "transparency") that would later turn them into risk-averse compliance bureaucracies.

---

* Seven people were killed in the autumn of 1982 when a murderer laced Tylenol capsules with cyanide in the Chicago area. The crime has never been solved.

The stakes were high in the 1990s, but the risks were comparatively limited. "Bring it on" was the ethic. Crisis managers were offensive players. We went on the attack and had good reasons to do so; spin doctoring hadn't yet become a "beat" where our talents had been inflated to meet the expanding journalistic need to fill expanding space.

During the brief heyday of damage control, most worthwhile private-sector crisis managers kept themselves *out* of the press in the same way that there had once been a time when nobody knew who Hollywood talent agents were, save the couple who threw big Oscar parties. Remaining behind the scenes worked well, not because we were doing anything sinister, but because vindication could not appear to have come about as the result of pressure, even if it was deserved. Nobody wanted things to degenerate to the point of the *Dateline*-GM fiasco. It was in everyone's self-interest for the right parties to come to their senses quietly.

The Case of the Invisible Victims

By the late 1990s, my firm was faced with a client challenge that was a portent of change. Rumors began to surface online that a client's feminine care product was injuring women. This was taken very seriously because in the early 1980s, dozens of deaths from toxic shock syndrome were attributed to tampon use. Reports began running in local markets, but there was one problem: Nobody could find the injured women.

Eventually investigative media outlets began digging and found that women weren't being hurt at all by these products; there was a start-up manufacturer of all-natural alternative tampons sending messages via computer to newsrooms across the country about women who had supposedly fallen ill. It was easier to spread false rumors about a rival consumer product than it was to compete with them in the marketplace. Once exposed, the controversy receded.

This was a new experience for us on a few levels. For one thing, there was the audacity of fabricating victims and thinking you could get away with it (which they did for a while). For another, there was the lack of rigor on the part of local media outlets to examine the information they were getting. They essentially were *forced* not to run these stories when the scam was exposed, and the likelihood of defamation actions became evident.

The same thing that happened with tampons happened on a more sustained basis with artificial sweeteners. Intensified by the spread of the Internet, in the late 1990s, an email from "Nancy Markle" began snaking its way around the Web stating that the sweetener aspartame (also known by the branded names NutraSweet, Equal, and others) caused Alzheimer's disease, multiple sclerosis, lupus, blindness, birth defects, and other debilitating diseases and conditions. The basis for these claims expressed in some email versions was the contention that the Food and Drug Administration approval process for the sweetener had been corrupted by sinister lobbyists.

The email, which took on life-of-its-own properties (soon to be known as "viral") that influence the aspartame safety debate to this day, is now universally regarded as a hoax. "Nancy Markle" appears not to exist; some experts on the hoax believe "she" is a pseudonym of a notorious cyber-crank who never encountered a chemical she couldn't affirmatively link to a scary disease.

In the 1980s and much of the 1990s, the average person didn't have a platform to capture attention. Controversy is now a race that anyone can run in. The send button on an email can inexpensively unleash a hurricane; the delete button can accomplish no equivalent task.

We've seen here how the media light never goes out, creating serious obstacles for targets of attack. Next we'll look at the content that fills this infinite time and space.

> **Takeaway:** The old weapons for managing controversies are obsolete because the new media terrain has little in common with the old. We cling to old notions about how the world works, leaving us to the perils of the present-day Fiasco Vortex.

3

"Monetizing Humiliation"

"Down these mean streets a man must go who is not himself mean..."

—RAYMOND CHANDLER

Let's look at the factors that catalyze the Fiasco Vortex. What is it exactly that makes it spin so much faster than it used to? The answers are some combination of the anonymous platform of the Internet, mass access to the tools of promiscuous leaking, a cultural fetish for self-promotion, social media's neutralizing effect on impulse control, and the rewards associated with trafficking in controversy.

In the past, if you were facing a damaging allegation, you could deny it, and the chances were that nobody could ever prove it. In the summer of 1983, a Los Angeles lawyer claimed that top Reagan administration officials were involved with a kinky sex ring. Washington chattered for a few days about who might be involved. I remember looking around the White House wondering who might be depraved, but hadn't landed on anybody. When top officials appeared to be shrugging their shoulders over the affair, the lawyer said he had a videotape. Seeing that the White House was unconcerned, the media said, "prove it." No videotape emerged. The story died.

Fast-forward a quarter century. During the 2008 presidential campaign, juggernaut candidate Barack Obama was blindsided when video footage emerged of sermons by his race-baiting pastor, Jeremiah Wright. If this man had been Obama's pastor for so long, the reasoning went, was it possible that Obama himself held such anti-white and anti-American views? Denying the existence of the sermons was not an option.

To take this to a new level of theoretical conspiracy, let's pretend that the Obama campaign had decided to pay the holder of the original footage to destroy it. Such an attempt would have failed because technology has snipped the wires in the brain that regulate self-control, and the owner of that tape would almost certainly have it stored on a computer somewhere. If my experiences in this area are any indication, he—or someone else with access to it—would have shared the footage anyway with the click of a send icon. In the Fiasco Vortex, there is no use in paying hush money when what you're trying to hush up is going to come out anyway.

The digital frontier has bred other forms of mischief that favor reiteration over recantation. Take this example from my own case files. A disgruntled employee planted a rumor on a minor blog that the FBI had raided his employer's offices and indictments were forthcoming. The blog was forwarded to a major newspaper I'll call the *Daily Bugle*. The *Bugle* began calling around the community where the employer, I'll call Copper, operated, setting off a cascade of rumors, blog posts, and comments on blog posts, most claiming to have some special insight into Copper's dirty deeds. This was a form of "push polling," a campaign dirty trick where a polling outfit plants negative or patently false information about an adversary disguised as a question in order to injure the adversary (e.g., "Does

Barack Obama's being a Muslim hatchet murderer make you more or less inclined to vote for him?").

That the authorities refused to comment about an investigation into Copper only served to confirm that there *must* have been an investigation in the works. While the *Bugle* never ran the story (because there wasn't one), a major online news site reported that the *Bugle* was "sitting on an explosive story" about Copper's impending criminal collapse. Another outlet reported "rumblings" of an investigation. The lesson here is that you don't even have to commit a crime anymore: Somebody can just murmur about it and cause terrible damage. This was a no-lose proposition for Copper's embittered ex-employee; some measure of injury was achieved, which was precisely the point. Copper survived, but the whiff of scandal cost them customers.

Media competition is so intense, as is the desire for media stardom, that it takes a lot less to make trouble for a target than it used to. Today, you don't need a blockbuster story for a takedown (although it helps); tweeting, surrogate tweeting, retweeting, and blog posts may do the trick.

We are confronting an entire generation of journalists who are not steeped in the traditions of journalism as much as they are in the traditions of celebrity-fueled career advancement. I spoke to a young magazine producer not long ago who informed me she had the "right" to see my client's confidential files on a particular subject. I expressed interest in what section of the Constitution addressed these rights. The answer I received was a hybrid of gibberish about the public's "right to know" and the "First Amendment." I informed her that I had been unaware that the Constitution had given her the authorization to plow through my client's proprietary documents, apologized for my ignorance, and asked her to kindly get back to me with more data on this matter of law. Crickets.

The subtext of this discussion was, "Look, I need a story, I need it fast, so give me what I need to knock off this target, and stop obstructing my Pulitzer destiny."

Anonymous Scourges

Another variable in the acceleration of the Fiasco Vortex is the increasing lethality of anonymous sources. Anonymous, or unnamed, sources have always been a problematic loophole in journalism. How do we really know the reporter *has* one? How can we judge the pedigree of the information if we don't know who these sources are?

Our journalistic and legal systems long ago determined that the broad benefits of anonymous sources outweighed the risks. Part of this assessment came from confidence in legacy media companies—a confidence that no longer exists. A newspaper such as the *Washington Post* had a lot to lose if it fabricated anonymous sources and, in fact, got in big trouble when a reporter, Janet Cooke, made up a Pulitzer Prize–winning story about a heroin-addicted eight-year-old boy in 1980.

With the proliferation of media and high-speed competition, standards have fallen, and anonymous sources can do unprecedented damage. The new players perceive they have either less to lose or much to gain.

The case of Heisman Trophy winner former Texas A&M quarterback Johnny Manziel demonstrates the power of anonymous sources. In August 2013, ESPN's *Outside the Lines* investigative show reported that Manziel was paid a significant fee for signing hundreds of autographs, which would be a violation of National Collegiate Athletic Association (NCAA) rules. All of the sources cited in the extensive coverage were anonymous, and none of them witnessed money changing hands. Manziel denied the allegations.

After a month of relentless news coverage, the NCAA cleared Manziel but gave him a half-game suspension for Texas A&M's first game. It's unclear what the suspension was actually for. The subtext of the coverage was that those reporting on the story didn't think it was possible that Manziel could have signed autographs for free. Never mind that Manziel comes from a wealthy family and may have signed the autographs because he was enjoying his newfound celebrity.

In the Fiasco Vortex, sometimes where there's smoke, there's just a smoke machine. But if the press gets their scoop and the public gets its gossip, the exercise is seen as being harmless.

Clickbait

In 1977, Ken Olsen, then the CEO of Digital Equipment Corporation, said, "There is no reason anyone would want a computer in their home." It seemed like a reasonable statement at the time. When I entered the workforce in the early 1980s, I had an IBM Selectric typewriter at my desk. A backspace button that whited out the last word typed was considered a brilliant invention. The fax machine came out a few years later and was a source of technological wonder: You fed a piece of paper in here, and seven minutes later it popped out somewhere far away in an inky scroll. Computers were gadgets that geniuses at NASA used. Technology advanced with a suddenness that is difficult to overstate and seminally altered the physics of controversy.

By the mid-1980s, computers were penetrating the home and office desktops, but they were still tools of isolation. The idea that most of us could communicate with *each other* via computers was, well . . . that was still NASA stuff.

By the late 1980s, an elite tier of people in the workplace could talk to each other via computers at their offices. By the mid-1990s, millions were regularly communicating with people *outside* our homes and offices via computer.

Today, nearly 80 percent of Americans are online. There are five billion Google searches each day. The amount of information we share online has multiplied nine times in the past five years. We upload 100 hours per minute of video footage to YouTube, up from almost nothing in 2007. Hundreds of millions of videos are shared every month on blogs and websites. Roughly a quarter of the time that Americans spend online is spent on social media. Facebook has well over one billion users (128 million in the United States), and there are 1,000 Facebook and Twitter posts per second. American Facebook users alone spend some 50 billion minutes a day on the site. Smartphone and tablet use are skyrocketing, rendering the creation and distribution of information virtually uncontrollable. The next wave of tech advancements will include devices that are wearable, are used in automobiles, and can be flown around for commercial purposes in the same way that "drones" are used in the military.

These innovations bring assets and liabilities to civilization. Being able to research and write this book from my laptop and telephone is a marvel. Following news stories online beats rushing to the *Washington Post*'s headquarters at five in the morning to see if my client is the target of a congressional investigation. Watching movies on my iPad makes exercise tolerable, and I prefer carrying my iPad on the train to lugging three hardback books aboard. Giving a succinct yes or no via email is better than suffering through the obstacles and distracting courtesies of trying to reach business associates by telephone or setting up unnecessary meetings.

On the liabilities side of the digital frontier is the Fiasco Vortex: my world of guiding clients through tempests. On this front, technology—the Internet, portable communications such as mobile telephones, tablets, and cameras, exponential news and entertainment media—has empowered critics and disarmed the mighty. As technology thinker Esther Dyson said, "The great virtue of the Internet is that it erodes power. It sucks power out of the center, and takes it to the periphery, it erodes the power of institutions over people while giving to individuals the power to run their own lives."

Dyson is right about the Internet redistributing power, but that power has troubling consequences out on the periphery. Now that it's so easy to become a scandal antagonist, it has led many to wrongly assume that crisis management is as easy as crisis creation. If you can blow somebody up with a few clicks, what can you do to parry this onslaught? The answer is that technology is inherently metastatic, not mitigating. Nevertheless, at our laptops, we are all journalists, cops, experts, celebrities, and crisis managers.

Diverse communications vehicles don't equate with diverse information flows. In controversies, what we actually see are extreme poles, diametrically opposed narratives dueling for informational real estate, and not very much in between. The content lurches between kill 'em or deify 'em, and when you're a big shot, kill 'em will win because technology conducts negative information more intensely and is resistant to mitigation. As defense attorney Mark Geragos has said, "The overwhelming percentage of rumors is not about what a good person the defendant is and how likely it is that he is innocent."

Editors and producers, the referees who once decided what was news, have been replaced by the tyranny of the click. A click occurs when you see an appealing feature being promoted online and select the hyperlink in order to read more. The slang for a sexy online news item is "clickbait." Clickbait is usually driven by online "story" headlines, which need not relate to story content. Internet news is replete with headlines suggesting that notorious murders have been solved, awful diseases are cured, and celebrity marriages are imploding, but the story content reveals nothing of the sort. No matter, it has been clicked.

Clicks are tracked and measured in order to determine advertising rates. The more clicks, the more the website or blog can charge advertisers. This is an electronic process that doesn't require the kind of seasoning, education, and judgment that media executives had. Simply put, the Internet knows what you're reading, tailors its news accordingly, and serves it back up to you as nano-stories that are quick, angry, and conclusive so you'll do more clicking.

A Wharton study on the most likely news stories to be circulated showed that "[m]ore anxiety- and anger-inducing stories are both more likely to make the most emailed list" of *New York Times* articles. A Massachusetts Institute of Technology study on Web traffic in China similarly concluded that, "the results clearly show that anger is more influential than any other emotions such as joy or sadness, a finding that could have significant implications for our understanding of the way information spreads through social networks."

Outrage fuels Internet discourse, thus the name given to those who search the Internet for fights to pick: trolls—those nasty little creatures who we were always told lived under bridges.

To stoke outrage, you need villains. Those villains are usually the powerful, but they are increasingly everyday people in tough situations, sometimes of their own making. The catharsis for this outrage can only come in the form of a takedown, which requires simple, declarative blocks of allegation. Anonymity gives attackers the confidence to ratchet up their rhetoric—independent of the truth—which serves as an accelerant to anger. It's easier to pick a fight when you're invisible than when you are face-to-face with someone who can hit you back. What's more, an online target of attack has no humanity; they're pixels, not people.

Provocative headlines and short articles are key clickbait components. When I've written articles for websites, editors have asked me to lighten up on the analysis and get quickly to opinionated conclusions. Online readers simply don't want to scroll down too far or have to click on a tab that takes them to another page where the article continues. It comes down to taking a clear position and sticking to it, which, in the context of controversy, means doling out blame and calling for a vivid punishment.

Perpetually in Our Faces

Resentment and frustration play an increasingly bigger role in what motivates attacks. As a boy, I only vaguely knew of the superrich. "Rich" was an orthodontist with a Mercedes. Today we have an unprecedented level of awareness of the outrageously successful. We can go on Google Earth and zoom in on the moat surrounding New England Patriots quarterback Tom Brady's 22,000-square-foot palace and then, hilariously, read feature stories about how environmentally friendly it is and how down-to-earth Brady and his supermodel wife are.

Baby-faced moguls mock us from the cover of business magazines. The Who Has the Biggest Yacht race is slugged out between billionaires Paul Allen and Larry Ellison for us online. We are all eminently aware that Gwyneth Paltrow's perfect life is a lot better than our flawed ones. There are more "power lists" than ever being published to remind us that we could live a thousand lifetimes and never meet anybody on the list, let alone be on it ourselves.

It is hard for a well-adjusted person not to feel like a loser when taking inventory of all we don't have, when we are constantly shown the career porn of Sheryl Sandberg and George Clooney. At least Sandberg and Clooney have achieved something, as opposed to the cavalcade of nonentities who populate the airwaves and magazine covers. If the Kardashians can achieve fame for nothing, why can't the rest of us?

Then there is the subtle competitive aspect of Facebook image-crafting, where we read about friends and acquaintances who appear to be doing excruciatingly well. People may be willing to post what cereal they had for breakfast, but it's less likely they will be merchandizing life's betrayals and disappointments.

I watched the insider-trading trial of management consultant Rajat Gupta with sadness because I imagined that a phenomenon might be at work in his case that I had seen with other white-collar defendants: the indignity of being worth only $50 million or $100 million when your friends are worth billions. All that hard work and still a nobody in your own mind. Tellingly, Gupta didn't even trade on his tips; rather his objective was to impress his billionaire friend Raj Rajaratnam that he, a board member at Goldman Sachs, was a big-time operator, too.

Meanwhile we are being bludgeoned with admonitions to be more charitable by people who give away more in a day than most of us will earn in a lifetime. Proselytizing charity is a welcome development, but during withering economic times when we fear for our futures, there is a backhanded implication that the rest of us have double-failed: Not only haven't we made a fortune in hedge funds or tech, but we also aren't giving enough money (that we don't have) away.

How could many of us not secretly rejoice when self-destructive actress Lindsay Lohan or Alex "A-Rod" Rodriguez are given everything and fling it back at the gods?

Another cultural factor in the metastasis of scandal is a broad-based desire for fame and notoriety. We are living in the age of the micro-celebrity where the ultimate disgrace is anonymity, not punishment for one's transgressions. In the past, a sense of shame and propriety kept scandal antagonists quiet. It is no accident that after all we have heard about John F. Kennedy's womanizing, comparatively few credible paramours have come forward to speak about it. There was once a sense that adultery was shameful. Contrast that with the sentiments of writer Erica Jong, who, after the Monica Lewinsky scandal broke, openly contemplated the thrill a woman might get from receiving a sexual souvenir of presidential DNA.

Had the Tiger Woods and Anthony Weiner scandals occurred in an earlier time, the chances are we would have heard very little about their women both because of the shame ethic and because there would have been limited venues for these women to strut. Several of the Tigresses, including porn stars and a pancake waitress, won six-figure deals from tabloids to tell their stories about Tiger, including sharing texts and emails. A few posed nude for magazines or made sex tapes, not a stretch given that some were porn stars to begin with. One became a "correspondent" for a tabloid TV show. A recipient of Weiner's crotch portrait, the outstandingly named Sydney Leathers, appeared in multiple media forums and won herself a porn contract.

Issue advocates such as the bikini-clad "Food Babe," a food industry watchdog, blogged her way into her own television show. There have been plenty of food activists over the years, but they tended to be researchers and scientists—and they *looked* like researchers and scientists. Food Babe was self-crafted for prime time, and it's publicity that powers food activism these days, not research.

One may just flip through television channels to see that more and more people cannot get enough of themselves as the desire for visibility has reached maniacal proportions. In years past, many of the ungifted contestants on talent competitions would have been ashamed to display their averageness before millions of people. Unless, of course, they actually think they have talent, which is even more troubling. From the Bravo *Real Housewives* franchise to romance competitions where contestants stand to be rejected before the world, visibility trumps antique notions of pride. As for VH1's *Mafia Wives*, it would appear that some within this once tight-lipped cohort are willing to put their lives at risk for a little airtime and a few bucks.

Of the teenagers in the 1950s who took a well-known personality test where one of the statements was "I am an important person," a paltry 12 percent agreed that it described them. As America approached the 1990s, 80 percent of teenagers answered this question in the affirmative. The cliché is that an obsession with self-promotion reveals latently low self-esteem, but the opposite may be true. Perhaps many are suffering from undeservedly *high* self-esteem and palliate the gap between fantasy and reality with excessive self-promotion on Facebook, Twitter, and self-portraits (known as "selfies") that are broadcast to a fan base that doesn't exist. It is the norm to "Like" something on Facebook simply because you've been asked to do so or because you don't want to offend the person who posted the item—not because you have genuinely been impressed by it.

Given that we've become a society starstruck on itself, most of these self-important people are going to be quite disappointed in the long run. Journalist Chris Heath summarized the phenomenon perfectly: "I'm not sure that we aren't seeing the emergence of a society in which almost everyone who isn't famous considers themselves cruelly and unfairly unheard."

In the recent past, players in controversies tended to keep an eye on the longer term. There was greater deliberation of the consequences of attacking someone you might need in the future. Given that paper and electronic correspondence is everywhere and can be compromised anonymously, there is less restraint on leaks. The emphasis of many parties in the age of the Twitter cycle is on the quick little kill.

During the October 2013 government shutdown, *Roll Call* reported that Senate Democrats were contemplating leaking the emails between the staffs of Senate Majority Leader Harry Reid and Speaker John Boehner. Senator Richard Durbin did not deny that this was being considered.

The communications construct here alone merits beholding:

1. Communicating the awareness of the *impulse* to leak;
2. Communicating the *impulse* to leak the *existence* of emails between the offices of the leaders of the most powerful nation on earth;
3. The willingness to throw under the bus the *staffs* of other members of Congress in a total breach of protocol;
4. The willingness to leak emails that most likely conveyed long-held positions that are not per se newsworthy;
5. The willingness to leak emails hoping that the very announcement of this impulse to leak (as opposed to actually leaking) them will result in a tactical victory;
6. Communicating the impulse to leak without consideration of the possibility that the opposition surely has emails of its own and can retaliate; and
7. Engaging in this adversarial behavior without considering the possibility that you may have to do business with your adversary in the future.

This affair marks the sanctification of short-term thinking. It also conflated the very possession of the documents of an opposing party with the possession of something scandalous. In the end, some of the emails were indeed leaked to *Politico*. The Democrats' gambit was rewarded as the Republicans were overwhelmingly positioned as the dirty players in the partisan wars.

Tom Cheney *The New Yorker Collection/The Cartoon Bank*

You Are the Enemy

Technology is the most efficient vehicle of irrevocable self-sabotage. Technology must lower the average IQ by about fifty points. Whatever dark impulses people have had from time immemorial, gadgets have been invented to seduce and capture our foibles for the world to behold. Some of my favorites:

- A young woman in the Delta Gamma sorority at the University of Maryland emailed her sorority sisters an expletive-laden rant accusing them of being "boring." The language is so vicious and profane (you can find it online, if you are interested, and you probably are) that one might conclude that being uninteresting is on par with genocide in College Park. Or not. The sorority quickly disassociated themselves from their psycho-sis, but the situation was reignited when the actor Michael Shannon, who is known for playing unhinged characters, acted out the letter in an online video;

- In 2008, a twenty-two-year-old Rhode Island man who had been arrested for a drunk driving accident that severely injured a woman posed for photos of himself at a party in striped prison garb emblazoned with the term "Jail Bird." Someone posted the photo of the gleeful party animal, who was holding a drink of indeterminate content, on Facebook. The prosecutor submitted the Facebook post to the judge, who agreed with the prosecution that the photos were "depraved." The young man was sentenced to two years in prison;
- Fraternity boys at Florida International University ran a criminal drug operation selling cocaine, Adderall, and marijuana-laced delicacies on Facebook, not to mention posted naked photos of underage girls. Concurrently, one of the frat's posts urged caution about what brothers should post on Facebook. Hmm. The fraternity has been suspended, and authorities are investigating;
- A group of teenagers illegally entered the vacation home of former NFL lineman Brian Holloway and vandalized his house, including a graffiti extravaganza and floors covered in alcohol and urine. The rapscallions, of course, took self-incriminating photos of their soiree and sent out hundreds of tweets containing commentary. Holloway identified the revelers on a website of his own. Holloway—the victim—is now facing lawsuits from the kids' parents angry that *Holloway's* actions may present troubles for their forthcoming college applications;
- In a poorly plotted slaying, thirty-one-year-old Floridian Derek Medina murdered his wife and uploaded the photo of her lifeless body onto Facebook, openly discussing his role in her murder. This is considered evidence in some circles;
- The driver of the Spanish train that crashed killing eighty people in 2013 had a history of posting on Facebook about his

derring-do. Francisco José Garzon Amo had once uploaded a photo of the speedometer of his train going 124 miles per hour, sweetening the post with, "I'm at the limit and I can't go any faster or they will give me a fine.... What a blast it would be to go parallel with the Guardia Civil [Spanish police] and go past them triggering the radar."

- A University of Iowa math teaching assistant accidentally emailed naked photos of herself to her students, who promptly tweeted about the incident. She had meant to send the students, eighty of them, guidance on a homework assignment. The photos were from a "cyber sexing" session she had been having with her boyfriend on an Internet video chatting service.

Twitter has been the vehicle for a number of instantaneous implosions and PR debacles, beginning with Congressman Anthony Weiner's tweeting of his crotch in May 2011:

- A CNN Middle East editor was fired for issuing a condolence tweet upon the death of a Hezbollah terrorist whom she "respect[ed] a lot";
- A St. Louis nonprofit executive was fired when her employer discovered via Twitter that she had been running a sex blog;
- A professor at East Stroudsburg University in Pennsylvania was suspended after two Facebook posts, one reading, "Does anyone know where I can find a very discreet hit man? Yes, it's been that kind of day," and the other, "Had a good day today. DIDN'T want to kill even one student";
- A Georgia police officer lost his job after posting his undercover activities involving a federal drug case, including the compromise of his schedule and frustrations with colleagues;
- Thirteen emergency room staffers at a Pennsylvania hospital were fired after participating in a racist group chat;

- In January 2012, McDonald's invited consumers to tweet about their special #McDonalds stories. This resulted in an avalanche of gross-out tweets such as, "Hospitalized for food poisoning after eating McDonalds in 1989. Never ate there again and became Vegetarian. Should have sued" and "Ordered a McDouble, something in the damned thing chipped my molar";
- In July 2012, a Burger King employee posted photos of himself online standing in tubs of lettuce in his dirty shoes along with the caption, "This is the lettuce you eat at Burger King." The culprit was tracked down within minutes and fired;
- Also in 2012, a Taco Bell employee tweeted a photo of himself urinating on a nacho plate and was swiftly fired;
- In November 2013, someone handling Home Depot's social media sent out a racist image on the company's Twitter account. The perpetrator was fired, and Home Depot apologized, but the episode succeeded in conveying the lack of control even savvy companies have over social media;
- In 2011, Qantas airlines paid dearly for inviting customer tweets about their favorite trips. At the time of this ill-conceived promotion, thousands of passengers were stranded overseas and were quite motivated to share their harsh assessments of flying Qantas; and
- Kellogg's apologized for a tweet implying that the company would feed hungry children if other Twitter users would retweet their promotion. While this hadn't been the intention of the company's message, the tweet left room for the interpretation that Kellogg's was tying humanitarian aid to promotional success.

"Revenge porn," whereby a disgruntled ex-romantic partner posts naked photos of his or her ex—and these photos are broadly distributed online to the point where they cannot be tracked or deleted—has become a veritable phenomenon. At least one revenge porn site was reportedly earning advertising revenues of ten thousand dollars per month. Said Danielle Citron, a University of Maryland law professor, "It's just an easy way to make people unemployable, undatable and potentially at physical risk."

The California state legislature has criminalized revenge porn, and there are increasing calls for federal action. At the moment, most laws protect the attacker because of the underlying issue of *consent*: Most of the victims of revenge porn either took their own compromising photographs or sent such photographs to the person who broadcast them. The law looks at this differently from other violations, such as when hackers creep onto computers and steal documents that the owner reasonably expected would remain private.

"It was only a matter of time before the Internet started to monetize humiliation," wrote David Segal of the *New York Times*. Now we have the publication of arrest mug shots on for-profit websites such as Mugshots, BustedMugshots, and JustMugshots. In fact, if you type a nonfamous person's name into a search engine and that person has an arrest record, the *top* search results will often yield their mug shot along with the charges. Wrote Segal, "The ostensible point of these sites is to give the public a quick way to glean the unsavory history of a neighbor, a potential date or anyone else. That sounds civic-minded, until you consider one way most of these sites make money: by charging a fee to remove the image. That fee can be anywhere from $30 to $400, or even higher. Pay up, in other words. . . ."

Simply because one website removes the photo, it doesn't mean another one is obligated to do so. Nor does it mean that a potential employer or garden-variety nemesis can't save the photo for future mischief. Major credit cards and PayPal accept payments for this service.

These are the consequences of enthusiasm about the value of a new technology without a careful analysis of its side effects. No one knows what new communications gizmos the future will bring, but they will surely expand the capacity for mischief that will make targets more vulnerable than ever.

> **Takeaway:** The speed of information, anonymous attack platforms, electronic provocation of resentment, gratuitous leaking, a rabid hunger for visibility, weak impulse control when interacting with social media, and the incentives placed on spreading damaging information have stacked the deck against attack targets to unprecedented degrees. Technology has made us more self-important, empowered, and promiscuous in our ability to injure targets.

4

Brittle—Why and How Goliath Became David (Part I—The Syndrome)

Man in Black (after defeating the giant, Fezzik): I do not envy you the headache you will have when you awake. But for now, rest well and dream of large women.

—*THE PRINCESS BRIDE*, WILLIAM GOLDMAN

In the spring of 2010, a handful of moms on Facebook registered complaints about the performance of reformulated Pampers "Dry Max" diapers. The product was wildly popular with consumers, but the Facebook moms were able to convey a broader sense of outrage than there really was by approaching media that were interested in covering online activism. The coverage contained the images of irritable babies with diaper rash, as if the common skin condition were a nascent scourge in human history brought on by this new product. Needless to say, close-up photos of infants' reddened skin are disturbing to look at. You want to blame somebody. Predictably, this attracted more Facebook moms, which added to the erroneous perception of broad-based consumer anxiety.

Plaintiffs' lawyers entered the fray and filed a class-action lawsuit. The coverage receded in large measure because of the popularity of the diapers and because there was nowhere else for the story to go once the Consumer Product Safety Commission found no link to diaper rash.

A little more than two years later, a U.S. appeals court threw out the settlement the plaintiffs reached with Pampers manufacturer Procter & Gamble because the class members were left "with nothing but nearly worthless injunctive relief." In other words, the only winners were the lawyers.

The Great Diaper Caper of 2010 illustrates the glass jaw phenomenon in the form of big companies known for resilience and innovation made vulnerable by a few motivated parties, and how those parties can be appropriated by savvy operators. *As with anything brittle, the term doesn't mean that the object will be destroyed beyond recognition or usefulness, but that it can be damaged or severely disrupted from its regular function—at great cost.*

The core operating principle of the brittleness syndrome is that a controversy expands in accordance with the number and resonance of the players who profit from its expansion. These players are often not powerful themselves, but sometimes those who start small can convert their grievances into a larger attack apparatus. Other times, a movement that appears to be a spontaneous "guerrilla" effort actually has vast resources.

Quick Pain

The Fiasco Vortex can be initiated or catalyzed by an entrenched "crisis creation" industry, including issue-driven NGOs, media, plaintiffs' lawyers, labor unions, short sellers, shareholder activists, bloggers, "wikiwarriors" (obsessive editors of Wikipedia entries), whistle-blowers, leakers, government watchdogs, publicity seekers, pundits, stalkers, and competitor-driven corporate fronts. In this dynamic, the meek are predators and the strong are prey.

In the two weeks after the 1989 crash and spill of the tanker *Exxon Valdez* in Alaska's Prince William Sound, Exxon's stock dropped 3.9 percent but quickly rebounded. In the month and a half after the 2010 spill in the Gulf of Mexico, BP's stock dropped 13.1 percent. Wrote energy analyst Pavel Molchanov, "For any given stock the response in the market for this type of news tends to be more sharp than it was 20 years ago," explaining to the *Wall Street Journal*, "Back in 1989, there were no bloggers... television news was dominated by the nightly network reports, and, in the markets, there was nowhere near the number of hedge funds, momentum traders, retail investors and electronic algorithms that add sharp reactions to negative news."

After 9/11, the concept of "asymmetric warfare," where under-resourced but determined attackers such as al-Qaeda could successfully injure much stronger targets like the United States, rightly fell into fashion. Al-Qaeda spent $500,000 to pull off 9/11 while the United States has spent $5 trillion in managing the aftermath.

The concept of asymmetric warfare has been applied to non-military challenges such as the capacity for hackers to penetrate and sabotage computer networks, power grids, and other vital interests. These things have already occurred. According to the head of the Center for Strategic and International Studies, the U.S. Departments of Defense, State, and Commerce, among others, were hacked by an agent of a foreign power in 2007. No one is certain how much information was taken, but the event was described as an "espionage Pearl Harbor."

While I want to caution against drawing the wrong conclusion here—that all smaller antagonists are terrorists—asymmetric warfare provides a conceptual template for why the seemingly small and powerless can injure the mighty regardless of their agenda, often at no cost.

The Industrialization of Leaking

Consider the handiwork of former government consultant Edward Snowden, who exposed the details of the sixteen U.S. government spy agencies, including the exact programs in its $52.6 billion "black budget." "Black" meaning secret. Or not so much. Among the programs made public, according to the *Washington Post*, were U.S. efforts to hack into foreign computer systems to sabotage and steal the secrets of other governments. Other embarrassing revelations included the monitoring of foreign heads of states' mobile phones, such as Germany's Angela Merkel. U.S. intelligence officials, concerned about the potential of leaks from government contractors like Snowden, had recommended reinvestigating these vendors. It is unclear whether these reinvestigations ever happened, but there is a mordantly ironic aspect of concerns about leaks being disclosed in a leaked confidential spy agency memo.

Nor were Snowden's disclosures mere embarrassments; they actually limited the intelligence community's freedom to operate after news reports and congressional hearings. After revelations about Merkel's mobile phone became public, Germany threatened to curtail some of its joint programs with the United States. Said Director of National Intelligence James R. Clapper, "The conduct of intelligence is premised on the notion that we can do it secretly, and we don't count on it being revealed in the newspaper."

All of this from one low-ranking government consultant who concluded, "I already won," by virtue of his disclosures.

Leaking documents used to be a rarer phenomenon. It

happened, sometimes to great effect, but not that often. It happens more today for the same reason that illegal music downloading was so prevalent in the late 1990s and early 2000s: Because we can.

Leaking used to be hard. So was stealing music. As a teenager, in the 1970s, stealing music would have meant my going into a local music store, where I knew people, and making off with a long-playing album, which was a cardboard container about twelve inches by twelve inches. There was nowhere to hide it and a huge likelihood of getting caught.

To leak documents in years past, it first meant accessing them. There simply weren't copies everywhere. So you needed to locate the document, remove it from a file cabinet or somebody else's office, and take it to be copied. There was a sense of thievery because you had to be conscious that you were doing something that you weren't supposed to.

Then you had to copy the document, which opened up more chances to get caught. You were likely to run into someone in the copier room. You had to make certain you knew how to operate the copier. And, if something jammed, you had a real problem on your hands because what if a page of the document ended up inside the apparatus? You could always come into the office at off-hours, but this, too, was conspicuous. The document then had to be returned, packed, mailed, or dropped off, which carried additional risks of being seen.

Not impossible, but not risk-free, either.

Even in a business as sensitive as crisis management, I am amazed by how many emails I receive containing strategic plans and other confidential papers that are copied to people I don't know. Some are probably employees of the client organization. Others are lawyers or consultants, but, as with illegally downloading music, there is a false sense of security when you are sending or receiving something from your own computer.

This delusion is compounded by an even worse one: the idea that everyone receiving the email or document is part of "the team." How can you possibly know if a random name on an email "cc" feels a fiduciary, moral, or ethical obligation to the principal? How do you know what people "on the team" will do to their fiduciaries, say, when they don't get the raise they want, and whether they will respect confidentiality obligations? The only people who I have found to be discreet about document exchanges are those who have been sued, publicly embarrassed, or suffered a personal loss associated with indiscretion.

What all of these things have in common is ease and propinquity. Just as illegal music downloading doesn't "feel" like a crime, flipping somebody a thumb drive or email doesn't feel like betrayal, even though it is. Furthermore, leaking has developed a certain élan. It's bold, hip, and stands for something. WikiLeaks founder Julian Assange described his objective as being "pain for the guilty": It's a win for transparency and keeping the Man honest. Plus, there is a certain thrill about seeing one's mischief find its way into a media forum.

How you feel about leaks, of course, depends largely on which side of the leak you are on.

Wolves in Activists' Clothing

Renegades can do more than leak; solitary players who are not household names now have unprecedented power to move financial markets. An accelerating trend in the markets is the use of the media by "shareholder activists." These activists sometimes "short" the stock in target companies (betting the stock will go down), go public with an attack on the company they are targeting by alleging malfeasance, and then enjoy the benefits of the negative coverage when the stock plummets.

In May 2012, well-known securities short seller David Einhorn asked a question on an earnings call for nutritional supplement firm Herbalife, which implied malfeasance and immediately trimmed the company's market value by one-fifth. In the months following, the stock lost about 40 percent of its value. The following year, it was reported that the Herbalife short position had been profitable for Einhorn's hedge fund, although specific figures were not disclosed.

In the Herbalife case, the attack on the company lay in its critics' conflation of its multilevel marketing (MLM) business model with a "pyramid scheme." While the two concepts resemble each other superficially, in that both feature the recruitment of additional salespeople in order to grow the enterprise, there is a fundamental difference. With MLM, salespeople are rewarded for both their own product sales and the sales of the people they recruit. In a pyramid scheme, participants are paid for the recruitment of others independent of whether these recruits actually sell products. MLM generates hundreds of billions of dollars in sales each year globally.

In a post-meltdown/Madoff era, people are understandably concerned about untrustworthy business practices. There is particular anxiety about business templates that are difficult to understand. After all, isn't that what derivatives and subprime loans were?

The problem comes when short sellers, media manipulators, plaintiffs' lawyers, and other crisis creators exploit an anxious operating environment and a limited understanding of business models in order to profit from a company's injury or destruction.

Another hedge fund manager, William Ackman, also began shorting Herbalife stock accompanied by a massive publicity campaign. In this effort, the same cadre of reporters from Einhorn's short hammered Herbalife and promoted their coverage through vehicles such as Twitter to the detriment of its share price. This process—shorting a stock and then hyping the short in the media—abets a self-fulfilling prophecy where the allegation serves as a proxy for meaningful evidence that something untoward is happening at the company.

All of these attacks were against a company that enjoyed more than fifteen straight quarters of growth.

In October 2013, Ackman began retreating from his short of Herbalife, which had won the backing of prominent financiers including Carl Icahn and Daniel Loeb. According to *Forbes*, Ackman's short cost his fund some $500 million as Herbalife shares rose 125 percent for the year. At this writing, Ackman maintains some of his short position.

There is nothing unlawful about any of this. Hedge fund managers enjoy the protections of the First Amendment, and reporters are allowed to serve as de facto PR agencies for sources and causes. There are no laws that prohibit having an agenda or requiring fairness. When clients on the receiving end of short attacks have asked me if I thought pro-short reporters were being paid for their advocacy, my answer has been *Sure, but not in the way you think*. It is unlikely that reporters for prominent media are receiving paper bags filled with cash by hedge fund managers. The compensation comes in the form of a steady stream of tips, story ideas, leaked data, and colorful interviews that advance the reporters' careers as hard-hitting journalists with Deep Throat–like access.

The Herbalife short illustrates the glass jaw phenomenon but with a twist: Sometimes a lone critic purporting to do a public good is actually a sophisticated and powerful operator who adorns the cloak of activism to profitable ends. In other words, David *is* Goliath.

Blowing the Whistle

There have never been greater incentives to take down your employer. In our quarterly-earnings-obsessed environment, the days of spending a whole career at one large company are mostly over. Corporations are loyal to their financial obligations, not their employees, and lay them off as conditions warrant. Employees are happy to return the sentiment with lawsuits, labor unions, moves to competitors, or just plain apathy.

Whistle-blowing, once a proposition that contained only risk and little reward, now can pay jackpots. I worked on a case where *one person* received $100 million from the government to expose the business practices of his employer. The award was a percentage of the overall mega-settlement. There have been a handful of whistle-blower awards in the nine digits and many more in the millions, not including book deals, speaking engagements, and new business ventures.

There are persuasive arguments to be made about the need to protect whistle-blowers. Companies are capable of doing bad things, but these levels of incentives beg the question, *Why would anyone bother to correct corporate misbehavior from within when the potential rewards for building a case against them are so much better?* This is especially true because there is a near certainty that if the federal government pursues the case, the company will pay a huge settlement (from which the whistle-blower award will be derived) rather than go to trial.

If big companies are so innocent, why don't they fight the government in court given their vast resources? Because, if there is even the smallest chance of being found guilty by a judge and jury, that company will be barred from doing business with the government. Given that most big companies work with the feds (think about drug companies being reimbursed by Medicare and Medicaid), no sane general counsel would allow a jury to decide the future of a multibillion-dollar enterprise with tens of thousands of employees. The same companies that have the financial power of nation-states can be reduced to mugging victims when a whistle-blower meets up with a motivated government agency and news media.

Perpetual Surveillance

Many scandal subjects need not wait for their enemies to attack them; they are adept at making themselves brittle. The Fiasco Vortex is not kind to those with weak impulse control. Indiscretions could once be denied or spun as having been taken out of context. Today there are photos, tweets, and witness testimony that make it hard for the biggest of big shots to take a punch to the jaw:

- CIA chief General David Petraeus was not undone by his affair with biographer Paula Broadwell. Lots of powerful people have had extramarital affairs, and their careers fared perfectly well. *Petraeus—who ran the nation's clandestine intelligence, no less—had corresponded with Broadwell via email.* He may have committed a moral and marital sin, but it was its electronic documentation that made his resignation inevitable. Boeing CEO Harry Stonecipher was similarly deposed after emails between him and an extramarital love interest surfaced;
- In September 2013, Robert F. Kennedy Jr., who kept a diary of his many extramarital sexual conquests and personal opinions of political leaders, saw its contents displayed in the *New York Post*. To make matters worse, this occurred about a year after his wife's suicide, which some of the tabloids had attributed to his infidelities;
- Oscar-winning actress Reese Witherspoon nicked her unblemished reputation when in April 2013 a police car camera captured her in a drunken rant at the patrol officer who had pulled her husband over for driving under the influence. Witherspoon herself was arrested for disorderly conduct. Among her less endearing statements was the threat to the policeman, "You're about to find out who I am."

- Witherspoon's was a dual violation because it contained both a threat to a police officer, which everybody knows not to do, and the ultimate American no-no: making a definitive assertion of a differentiation in class status. Witherspoon delivered a sincere and mortified apology in a television interview. Still, the original police video that displayed Witherspoon's dark side lives on for eternity.

- *Seinfeld* star Michael Richards's moment of mortification came during a 2006 standup performance at the Laugh Factory club where he responded to hecklers with a racist epithet. The outburst was picked up on a cell phone camera. Richards apologized and later admitted the incident was one of the reasons he has stopped doing live performances;

- Maryland attorney general and gubernatorial candidate Douglas Gansler was captured on a cell phone camera in the middle of an out-of-state beach party where underage drinking was taking place. He had been an advocate for cracking down on underage drinking. Gansler's explanation was that he had simply been checking in on his teenage son, not partying himself. This is likely true, but the photo is easily misinterpreted, portraying Gansler partying at worst and ignoring behavior that he once admonished at best. Even if he is given the benefit of the doubt, Gansler had to face questions about why he didn't take action as a parent to stop the party;

- Former National Security Agency chief Michael Hayden was embarrassed when his background briefing with reporters via telephone on an Acela train was overheard by a political activist who proceeded to live-tweet what he was hearing along with commentary. The information included tidbits about President Obama's hack-proof BlackBerry and CIA "black sites." The tweeter, Tom Matzzie, alleged that

Maryland Attorney General Douglas Gansler. Instagram

Hayden had been disparaging the Obama administration, which Hayden denied. Regardless, it was a bad situation for Hayden, one that would have been unlikely to occur in real time pre-Twitter;

- An Obama White House national security aide working on disarmament negotiations with Iran was fired when he turned out to be the "mystery tweeter" sending out highly sensitive material and profane criticism of administration officials, journalists, and political adversaries, including jabs at their intelligence and slovenly appearance. Among them: "Look, (Republican Rep. Darrell) Issa is an ass, but he's on to something here with the @HillaryClinton whitewash of accountability for Benghazi" and "Loved, LOVED the @NYTimesDowd column eviscerating the Clintons today. @ChelseaClinton seems to be assuming all of her parents' vices...";

- Justine Sacco, a top communicator at media company IAC, was fired after tweeting, "Going to Africa. Hope I don't get AIDS. Just kidding. I'm white!";
- Pax Dickinson was ousted as chief technology officer of *Business Insider* after he went one tweet too far about the competence of women in technology; and
- Actor Alec Baldwin has had repeated spontaneous combustions against paparazzi, documented by photos, tweets, and videos. In fact, provoking celebrities like Baldwin and Sean Penn in order to get footage of them exploding is an old paparazzi trick that has taken on a new velocity because of the instantaneous communications available to merchandize these outbursts.

The standard advice for managing this phenomenon is some amalgam of: 1) "always remember there are cameras everywhere"; 2) "be careful what you put in email or on Facebook/Twitter"; and 3) "don't keep a diary," or, in the case of former congressman Anthony Weiner, "don't take and broadcast photos of your own private parts."

The problem with this advice is that everybody who gets in trouble through these means *already* "knows better," but they do it anyway. Richard Nixon—no dummy—kept audiotapes of his discussions during the height of the Watergate cover-up and didn't even destroy them when he knew the investigations were heating up.*

Today, incidents of memorialized self-immolation continue to multiply for the famous and unfamous alike. What makes today's surveillance different is its ubiquity and leakiness. Using prolifer-

---

* Presidents Franklin Roosevelt, Eisenhower, Kennedy, and Johnson also kept recordings. In all of these cases, the recordings were made at their direction with the presumption of absolute custody and discretionary release, which was possible in those days.

ating technology, with all of its risks, has become an autonomic function, such as breathing—occurring below human consciousness. While it would be ideal to summon the ability to always be on guard, it's not going to happen.

Once you tell a compulsive self-saboteur to stop being a compulsive self-saboteur, there isn't much else you can do. I have had hundreds of encounters with people and institutions that are explicitly warned about certain high-risk exposure, and these warnings have an effect on a small fraction of them. You cannot educate people beyond their life experience and impulses, and if someone doesn't already know that purposely transmitting nude selfies to other people is problematic, a consultant's wisdom is worthless.

Occasionally, a high-risk personality can benefit from a "handler" who protects them from volatile situations. Professional athletes in particular can be restrained at the margins by team security and public relations people, but this trick works better in the movies than it does in real life. Strong personalities don't tolerate handlers well, and it's only a matter of time before they find a way to ditch them. For every person in comic John Belushi's orbit who tried to keep him away from drugs, there were lines of pushers and enablers up and down Sunset Boulevard who were all too pleased to provide him with the drugs that would kill him. The same applies to PR overdoses.

A Perverse Protection Racket

As a kid, I once saw an uncomfortable conversation between a store owner and a rough-looking customer. I described the incident to an uncle, who explained that what I likely observed was a local hoodlum offering "protection" to the merchant. In all likelihood, the "customer" was telling the merchant that if he didn't pay him a certain amount of money, the store—and perhaps the owner himself—would be harmed.

I wondered whether paying a monster like this wasn't such a bad idea if he was actually providing protection services.

I have thought about this concept often as I have watched prominent individuals and organizations paying "protection" to those who come calling not with baseball bats but with earnest smiles and allusions to noble causes. The twist is that these smiley-faced protectors—race hustlers, community activists, corporate critics—accept money with one hand *and* clobber the mark with the other, which violates the core principle of protection racketeering.

In a presentation to a consumer products company under siege over a safety issue, I discussed the extensive backing of the organizations attacking them. "Who is funding them?" one executive asked. "You are," I answered. Indeed, they had been, openly, under the aegis of supporting good causes. There was a lot of uncomfortable shifting around the meeting table. I assumed that some of the participants felt they had been exposed for their activism gambit.

You are supposed to give the local hoodlum a monthly stipend so that he *doesn't* burn down your store. The problem comes when you give him money and he still burns down your store. Is any corporate flack going to confront a media-connected NGO it gave money to and demand an explanation for why it took their money and attacked them anyway? Doubtful. That would trigger an investigative report in which the company would play the villain role even though the company is the victim in the transaction. Better to just keep paying, the reasoning goes, because your tormentor is now your partner.

Institutional masochism plays out on a broader, less transactional level as well. Huge charitable foundations such as Pew, Ford, Rockefeller, and Carnegie fund initiatives that attack the interests of their creators. When Henry Ford II resigned from the Ford Foundation in 1976, he wrote in his resignation letter, "The system [capitalism] that makes the foundation possible is very probably worth preserving."

Among other recipients, the Ford Foundation has contributed to the Jerusalem Media and Communications Centre, which has promoted groups labeled as terrorists such as the Popular Front for the Liberation of Palestine, Hamas, and Islamic Jihad.

A great deal of Big Foundation money goes to public interest law firms, which attack the very interests that funded their origins. These firms are tax-exempt because they are not seen as political advocates even though their impact is extremely political.

The Nathan Cummings Foundation, established by the free-market founder of Sara Lee, the food conglomerate, has supported causes such as tax hikes on corporations and high-net-worth individuals, shareholder activism, and labor initiatives, including some against the food industry. Cummings's CEO was a former labor organizer.

The Rockefeller Foundation, which was set up by oil magnate John D. Rockefeller, has supported causes such as the Tides Foundation, a foe of the petrochemical industry. Rockefeller has also given grants to the antibusiness U.S. Public Interest Research Group and the powerful Service Employees International Union's (SEIU) Education & Support Fund. Among other initiatives, SEIU was active in the Occupy Wall Street movement. One of the union's lead organizers promised to "bring down the stock market" through a campaign of chaos.

These examples just scratch the surface of the financial, political, and cultural might of those allied against increasingly frangible business interests.

During the financial crisis, where giant banks were rightly criticized for giving out risky loans to borrowers who could not pay them, a lesser-known factor was the role that public interest groups such as Association of Community Organizations for Reform Now

(ACORN) played in demanding that those loans be awarded in the first place.

Many NGOs are full-time attack organizations that position themselves as Davids up against asset-rich Goliaths. This is validated in issue combat by citing a company or industry's sales figures. After all, how could a merry band of do-gooders ever fight an entity with billions in sales? The counterintuitive reality is that issue-warriors focus far more resources to attack a target than that target is willing to devote to defending itself. Corporations are organisms constituted to manage sales, not threats. Their critics are built to threaten. In a company, any diversion of resources—human, financial, political—is a disruption to the enterprise—overhead that drains the sales engine.

Animal rights groups have war chests in the hundreds of millions of dollars solely devoted to advocacy. The largest corporations in the world with interests in animal testing, such as pharmaceuticals and cosmetics, spend about fifty thousand dollars on average to contest their opponents, according to the Foundation for Biomedical Research.

We are accustomed to thinking of critics of the powerful as well-meaning but unsophisticated citizens. This archetype goes back to the founding of the United States by republican activists. This notion has a basis in reality, a positive template that has led to some of the greatest social achievements the world has ever known: democracy, civil rights, improved working conditions, to name a few.

The Fiasco Vortex demands that we update our conception of the provenance of criticism. In addition to the increasing asymmetry of controversy, many ostensibly weak parties have become imposing conventional forces. As with ancient guerrilla campaigns, issue-warriors benefit from outside assistance. We are in the midst of an unprecedented corporatization of dissent. No longer are crisis principals dealing with a hodgepodge of crusaders but well-financed adversaries who possess the moral authority of underdogs.

On environmental issues, the assets of anti-business environmental groups overwhelm those proposing free-market solutions by about 250 to 1. The war on genetically modified organisms (GMOs) in food has been framed for more than two decades as a fight between Big Agriculture and small organic farmers. On the contrary, wrote *Forbes*: "A review of tax returns of the 'non-profit' activist organizations opposing agricultural biotechnology and other modern methods reveals more than $2.5 billion is being spent annually in the USA by these professional advocacy groups to shape our beliefs and influence our purchasing habits."

YOUR CHALLENGE IS SOMEONE ELSE'S MEAL TICKET

Media

Competitors

Bloggers

Your Crisis

Plaintiffs' Bar

Activists

Politicians

Whistle-blowers

Short-Sellers

Prosecutorial Maestros

The loose confederacy of crisis creators comprises plaintiffs' lawyers, powerful NGOs, and the news media. Plaintiffs' lawyers often initiate controversies, NGOs certify their significance, and the media retail them to broader audiences.

This process requires no meetings in alleyways where sacks of cash are exchanged with dodgy reporters. These are *not* conspiracies. They are a long-entrenched form of phototropism, the process whereby plants naturally bend toward the sunlight that nourishes them. The plants aren't conscious of bending; it's just what they do. Crisis creators simply need one another, and they have worked well together for a long time. It is common for members of Congress (and staff) to partner with like-minded NGOs and plaintiffs' lawyers in order to gather and share intelligence on their targets through subpoenas so that these simpatico parties can leverage the information in their everyday business.

In 2011, the *Wall Street Journal* reported on the rise of venture capitalists placing bets on litigation and how "the new breed of profit-seeker sees a huge, untapped market for betting on high-stakes commercial claims. After all, companies will spend about $15.5 billion this year on U.S. commercial litigation...." One litigation entrepreneur reports that it "looks for cases with a potential recovery of $25 million or more on investments of $1 million to $10 million." There is a burgeoning industry of "lead generators" who sell lists of purported victims to plaintiffs' lawyers for $500 to $2,000 per name. Even prestigious data companies such as LexisNexis promise trial lawyers they can quickly "fill your new business pipeline with pre-qualified legal leads."

Wrote David Callahan in *Fortunes of Change*, "Most lawyers who make a few million dollars a year are in firms that mainly do corporate work. If you want to get seriously rich, you need to be on the other side of the fence, suing corporations and insurance companies."

Plaintiffs' attorneys and prosecutors make promiscuous use of the news media, a bully pulpit that their targets rarely have. In nearly all of the cases where I consult with defense counsel, we are playing, well, defense. Prosecutors recognize that media intrinsically favor their narratives, which is why they parade high-profile defendants before the cameras in "perp walks." If they thought there was any chance the defendants would be covered favorably, or that the public would be skeptical of their charges, they wouldn't stage perp walks, hold news conferences, or tip off friendly journalists about ongoing investigations.

It is only on rare occasions that prosecutors have to show restraint with a perp walk. A reporter who was covering the Martha Stewart insider trading scandal called me shortly before her arraignment for background color about what might happen at the actual event. "So, I guess we'll have the usual perp walk," he said.

"I'd be stunned if they perp-walked Martha," I said.

The reporter was surprised. "Really? Why?"

"The prosecutors are smart enough to know that the optics of a bunch of big, scary cops restraining a woman is bad stagecraft," I explained. "They'll take her through an underground entrance or something."

And this is exactly what happened. This was not an impressive psychic projection on my part. My assessment had simply been a function of experience—my own and others.* The prosecutors simply realized that the perp walk was a poor device for this particular occasion.

---

* I reminded the reporter of what happened when Congressman Rick Lazio ran against Hillary Clinton for Senate in 2000. During a televised debate, he physically approached her at her podium, which conveyed as a gender-relevant bullying maneuver. A similar principle applies to perp-walking a female defendant.

Attorneys Mark Geragos and Pat Harris wrote in their book *Mistrial* about how prosecutors will lay out their entire case against a defendant in a press conference. "Then, when the defendant hires an attorney, the prosecution will file a motion with the court to issue a gag order for both sides as if they are trying to be fair. This way they can be the final word anyone hears on the case."

Even when prosecuting bodies are silent, they broadcast guilt. As we saw with the Copper example, the statement "we do not comment on ongoing investigations" suggests that there *is*, in fact, an ongoing investigation. This leaves the rest to the power of the imagination, which instinctively gravitates to guilt. The presumption of innocence is a legal premise, but it has no relationship to the human drive for a public curiosity or catharsis.

The intrinsic nature of media coverage is to facilitate mob justice, which operates on speed. Conversely, the intrinsic nature of most defense work is to urge deliberation, which is slow-moving. This is why defense teams rarely leak to the press their suspicions of investigations into their clients. Rather they default to "no comment" or, if an arrest or indictment comes down, they state that the charges are unfounded and that they are confident of vindication in court.

When news reports cite investigative targets and cover arrests and indictments, it makes it harder for defendants to pursue charges of defamation because the harmful allegations don't *originate* with the press. Coverage either emphasizes public statements by law enforcement, repeats the content of court filings—which are larded with juicy charges—or uses weasel words such as "reputed" or "alleged," terms that convey guilt with a wink.

If defense counsel seeks to push back, reporters ask what the basis for their grievance is. This would require counsel to lay out their case to someone they cannot trust during a time when they are building their client's defense and still learning the facts. In the absence of a catastrophic weakness in the prosecution's case, the defense is mostly defenseless on the media front.

When he was attorney general of the state of New York, Eliot Spitzer was particularly adept at gaining favorable news coverage for his prosecutions and shakedowns of influential businesses. The press reliably ran Spitzer's targets (a few were clients of my firm) through a buzz saw. With few exceptions, major media, seeking scalps, covered the investigations as if Spitzer had written the stories himself. The negative attention and all that it wrought was unsustainable; with few exceptions, it was impossible to mitigate the reputational damage against the backdrop of prosecution. No legal counsel would risk the future of venerable corporations to the caprice of a jury. Nearly all of Spitzer's targets settled and paid out settlements totaling in the billions, including Samsung, Goldman Sachs, Deutsche Bank, Credit Suisse, and J.P. Morgan. The accused, of course, can be guilty, but Spitzer-style tactics make demonstrating innocence a profound challenge.

Don't defense attorneys brief the media? Yes, but more often than not, defendants simply want their problems to go away and rarely benefit from provoking additional cycles of news. The exception lies when there are egregious vulnerabilities in the prosecution's case, such as in the Duke lacrosse case, where a preposterous victim falsely accused several young men of rape and was abetted by an ambitious prosecutor. The prosecutor was ultimately disbarred. The accuser was herself recently convicted of murder.

The Speaking Complaint

Perhaps the most influential crisis creators are plaintiffs' attorneys, and many of their talents are displayed outside of court and in new and old media. Lawsuit complaints are worded to maximize media coverage and social media access. Many of the lawsuits we are seeing in my practice are little more than publicity stunts to injure targets in order to accomplish an extralegal objective such as fund-raising, political point-scoring, or marketplace advantage.

Colorfully worded filings are referred to as "speaking complaints" because they are designed for maximum PR leverage. A speaking complaint helps journalists friendly to plaintiffs' lawyers write lurid stories with a reduced fear of being sued because the media are simply reporting the contents of a legal complaint filed with a court.

But wouldn't plaintiffs be embarrassed to file lawsuits that end up being dismissed or lost outright? Not when the media can be counted upon to report the filing of the lawsuit with sympathetic fanfare and its dismissal at a minimum or not at all. This modus operandi is the norm.

It is in the spirit of this syndrome that media outlets can accept inestimable in-kind services in the form of story origination, leaks, research studies, whistle-blowers, and staged events by antagonists they either agree with or who make good copy, and it raises no hackles. Activist billionaire George Soros has funded approximately 180 media organizations, to the tune of about $48 million. High-ranking journalists from thirty major news organizations sit on Soros boards, a subject of interest to a tiny cohort that follows such things. But if a company under attack pays a toxicologist a few thousand dollars to vindicate a product's safety, she is either dismissed with a snarl as a shill for industry or finds herself a target of ethics complaints at her university.

The appetite by investigative media to examine plaintiffs' lawyer funding and the agendas of issue-driven NGOs is limited to nonexistent. When, for example, an activist group criminally obtains information from a corporate target, those data are reported in the press without regard for their origin (e.g., "documents obtained by the *Daily Herald*"). If, however, the target attempts to supply the press with information about its critics, the story is likely to focus on dirty tricks by sinister entities, even if the techniques used in the process were perfectly legal.

In the eyes of the corporate target, it is rarely worth the risk of even pursuing such a strategy, knowing how badly it is likely to turn out.

Here we examined the conditions that render big shots brittle. Now we will look at the mentality that exacerbates this syndrome.

> **Takeaway:** One person's crisis is another's meal ticket. The systemic incentives associated with crisis creation conspire to bring giants to their knees.

5

Brittle—Why and How Goliath Became David (Part 2—The Mindset)

"We grow tired of everything but turning others into ridicule, and congratulating ourselves on their defects."

—WILLIAM HAZLITT

A famous investigative reporter once asked me why my corporate clients were so terrible at defending themselves during controversy. I explained, "It's not what they *do*. Companies make and sell stuff. They don't fight critics for a living. And they dread the very idea of a fight. Critics criticize; it's their entire purpose for existing; it's what *they* do."

"But the companies have all that money!" he said, exasperated.

"But their critics have *you*," I said.

The conversation ended.

My point was that companies are so psychologically traumatized by the very prospect of controversy that many of the battles they may face are over before they begin. This mindset has four pillars: denial, avoidance, surrender, and expedience. It also has a basis in functional reality. In addition to the drain on financial resources, companies don't have all day to sit around fighting issue-warriors and the "bathrobe brigade," the diffuse army of millions who wage war on the world from their kitchen table laptops at no cost. Their critics are able to make decisions about prosecuting attacks in a fraction of the time it takes big organizations to figure out how to respond or whether to respond at all.

Companies are simply not set up to manage crises either mechanically or constitutionally, whereas their adversaries are. Corporate and institutional critics have passion, will, and the cloak of virtue. They *want* the attack to remain in perpetuity. Their targets, conversely, have a different mindset: They are motivated by institutional tranquility—they want the enterprise to keep humming along, quietly paying dividends and maintaining job security.

Despite the prevalence of corporate sales meetings that traffic in the conceit that executives are barrier-busting rebels, most corporate people find fights with issue-warriors to be distressing on a personal level and resist participating. This can be because of a basic sympathy with the critics' positions, concern about doing anything that could escalate tensions, or a fear of the career consequences of being in the line of fire. I have been in hundreds of meetings and on phone calls with large organizations under siege, and the prevailing theme of these sessions is JUST MAKE IT STOP. Put differently, it is in no one's self-interest to make a broader organizational challenge one's own personal jihad, to try to preserve the organization more than it cares to preserve itself.

When it is under attack, an institution is little more than a collection of individuals angling for self-preservation. No one's mental framework includes a career arc that places them in the middle of a Fiasco Vortex during a climate when there are dozens of data points that will be leaked or otherwise surface in discovery or depositions. One corporate client likened being on a crisis management team to being a character in William Golding's *Lord of the Flies*, never knowing which of his colleagues may end up killing him. His corporate enemies were gently nudging him into the spotlight hoping that if he became the face of the crisis, he, not they, would take the fall.

Conventional wisdom would suggest that if a subordinate is ordered into battle, he would instinctively comply. Never underestimate the stubbornness of an entrenched bureaucracy; if the rank and file are resistant to joining a fight, inertia has more staying power than a boss's obsession-of-the-moment. As Admiral Hyman Rickover said, "If you are going to sin, sin against God, not the bureaucracy. God will forgive you but the bureaucracy won't."

Big companies are increasingly becoming compliance organizations where the mission profile is to avoid risk. Busywork PR initiatives and self-congratulatory rhetoric often serve as proxies for meaningful action or sedatives to take the edge off the fear of an initiative blowing up. It is reminiscent of the escapades in Joseph Heller's *Catch-22* where pilots would drop bombs in the desert or in the ocean rather than on enemy targets just to *appear* to have fulfilled their missions, as opposed to actually putting themselves in harm's way.

Then there is the "quant" mentality that pervades companies. Endeavors have to be measurable to be justified; there must be a "return on investment" (ROI). I know we're going to have an expectations problem when, at the outset of a controversy, someone asks me for a list of "deliverables" and wants assurances on what the company is going to get for their money. The challenge with crisis management, however, is that it saps overhead, the ultimate unanticipated cost, and not a small one. Moreover, the nature of crisis management is to mitigate badness, not increase sales, the way one would anticipate with an investment like advertising. No one sees it as being in their self-interest to commit themselves (and their overhead) to a lose-by-a-little-less proposition. It's easier to get another $10 million for an advertising campaign than $100,000 to try to put out a fire. Economists refer to this as "hyperbolic discounting," where perceived immediate benefits trump remote intangible ones.

Symbols Drive Narratives, Not Data

A "social responsibility" PR firm sent out a blast email in mid-2013 touting the success of their campaign to get people to wear "hoodies" to protest the acquittal of George Zimmerman on murder charges in the slaying of Trayvon Martin. Martin had been wearing a hooded sweatshirt when Zimmerman killed him after a scuffle. The garment became an instant symbol of the tragedy.

The intrinsic narrative at work here—an unarmed teenage black man killed under circumstances that did surely not warrant a death sentence—begs the question of how much PR wizardry was really needed to pull off these hoodie protests. Even though Zimmerman was found not guilty of Martin's murder, it would be difficult for a sane person to conclude that this chain of events was something other than a tragedy.

Persuading the media to cover victims sympathetically is about as challenging as persuading parents to love their newborn baby. From a cold communications perspective, "hoodies for Trayvon" is a much easier sell than, say, "hoodies for Dow Chemical" would be. Just because a groundswell occurred doesn't mean somebody engineered it or that it can be replicated. The hoodie was shrewdly appropriated as a symbol in the same manner that environmentalists seized the "garbage barge" that cruised the east coast in the late 1980s as a symbol of an America drowning in garbage. This vivid symbol ignited solid waste legislative battles that raged for years even though the "buried alive" idée fixe that captivated the culture has long slipped from public consciousness.

The theologian Paul Tillich said that a symbol "participates in that to which it points." Symbols and other forms of shorthand tend to emerge organically but can be exploited strategically. Comedian Chevy Chase portrayed President Gerald Ford on *Saturday Night Live* as a hopeless klutz. Ford, who had taken two falls but was one of our country's most athletic presidents, could never shake the image, and it became shorthand for an inept presidency.

Jimmy Carter soon defeated Ford. Carter himself collapsed with a flourish enabled by an iconic photo of him beating back a "killer rabbit" with a canoe paddle. The high-strung rabbit had accosted him while boating. The episode became a caricature of Carter's feckless presidency.

Manhattan's Central Park became shorthand for defiled tranquility when five men were falsely accused of a brutal assault and rape in the late 1980s. The archetypes of dark-skinned hoodlums, dubbed the "Central Park Five," raping a white woman in the sacred domain converged during a time of high crime and racial tensions against the backdrop of gaudy affluence in Manhattan.

In 2008, at the height of the financial crisis, the private jet became a meme of oblivious privilege when the CEOs of the Big Three automakers, General Motors, Ford, and Chrysler, were pilloried for traveling to Washington in corporate airplanes to plead for a government bailout. Never mind the inefficiencies of having leaders responsible for millions of people and hundreds of billions of dollars spending their days in airport lines futzing with their shoes; the optics triumphed.

In December 2013, Organizing for Action, a group supportive of ObamaCare enrollment, tweeted a photo of a bespectacled hipster in his pajamas nestling a mug and the admonition, "Wear pajamas. Drink hot chocolate. Talk about getting health insurance." On the heels of the perilous ObamaCare launch, "Pajama Boy" became a symbol for ridicule, not enrollment, the takeaway being that the Obama policymakers were preaching to their own elite tribe or were seeking to remake Americans into precious elves wearing ironic glasses and arch expressions.

Verbal statements become cultural memes as well. Goldman Sachs's CEO, Lloyd Blankfein, stated that his bank was "doing God's work" during the financial crisis, which portrayed his firm as being above reproach amidst allegations of rapacity.

President George W. Bush's congratulation to Federal Emergency Management Agency chief Michael Brown for "doing a heckuva job, Brownie" during the aftermath of Hurricane Katrina in 2005 certified that Bush's administration was oblivious to the true state of the catastrophe unfolding in New Orleans.

BP chief Tony Hayward remarked that he "wanted his life back" during the cleanup of the 2010 oil spill in the Gulf of Mexico, which conveyed self-pity in the wake of a catastrophe that did so much damage.

Candidate Obama's campaign foundered in 2008 when he was captured on audiotape offending a large swath of the population, dismissing those who "cling to guns or religion." This reinforced Obama's reputation as a cultural elitist. Candidate Mitt Romney's 2012 bid was hobbled by his statement that 47 percent of Americans would vote for Obama because they are dependent upon the government and wouldn't take responsibility for their lives, which further positioned him as a plutocrat.

All of these things resonated because the words were faithful to events and beliefs and human reactions to them. The incidents triggered a preexisting intuition that "I always knew this was the kind of person/organization [insert principal] was."

A Cultural Sea Change

After the changes in communications technology, perhaps the biggest transformation I've witnessed in how corporations confront controversy is how the people inside companies view themselves. It is a cultural sea change where there is a gnawing suspicion that capitalism is bad and that the critics of capitalist enterprises are right to be hostile to them.

I went to college in the early 1980s, the heyday of the movement to boycott companies engaged in controversial behavior. A major example of this was campus pressure to divest from companies that did business in South Africa. This period was the aftermath of Love Canal (late 1970s, the pollution of an upstate New York community), the accident at the Three Mile Island nuclear reactor (1979), and the campaign against Dow Chemical, the manufacturer of the incendiary chemical napalm that was used in Vietnam. While the use of napalm had been known for some time, the full debate about its effects became most intense in the late 1970s, and the United Nations finally banned its use in 1980.

We saw the Ford Pinto catch fire and explode, killing dozens of people, in a 1977 *Mother Jones* exposé, and saw the interviews with a horribly disfigured man, a human symbol of what happens when corners are cut. Ralph Nader became a cultural icon, and we heard the stories about how General Motors spied on him and tried to gather information about his sex life when he was exposing safety secrets about the Chevrolet Corvair. There were the boycotts against Nestlé for its marketing of infant formula in third-world countries, which critics alleged was a health hazard to babies. The movie *Silkwood*, about antinuclear activist Karen Silkwood, starring Meryl Streep, came out in 1983 and earned Streep an Academy Award nomination. The film left the impression that Silkwood's corporate employer killed her because of her activism. This is probably false, but the culture got the message.

My generation was weaned on Watergate, the Pentagon Papers, and tales of a Kennedy assassination conspiracy, and anyone who had the slightest claims to coolness not only "knew" that the CIA killed the president, but we knew why: Kennedy was going to get us out of Vietnam, and the hidden cabal that truly controlled America wanted the war to continue. I remember being able to point on a photograph to the shrubbery near the grassy knoll where the "real" shooter had pulled the trigger. I knew that this was the place because you really couldn't see anything there, which was proof that the shooter was *that good*. One friend was sure that Nixon gave the order, presumably because this was the kind of thing Nixon did, even though he was working at a law firm at the time, the perfect cover.

Perhaps the most grotesque proof that the Bastards (as a shaggy-haired camp counselor called them) were out in full force were the photos of the children who had been deformed by the morning sickness drug thalidomide in the late 1950s and early 1960s. There was a book in my local library that was always checked out because it contained photos of these poor kids that were so disturbing that we had no choice but to keep looking at them in order to give ourselves nightmares. This was a badge of social consciousness.

Fast-forward thirty years, and my crowd is firmly in charge of corporate America and the government. (President Obama was in college at the same time I was.)

The culture ultimately triumphs, and we cannot ignore the seminal narratives of our coming of age. *Nobody wanted to grow up and become one of the Bastards.* Even if we came to disbelieve that Mobil Oil had tankers hovering out at sea in order to artificially drive up the price of gasoline during the oil embargo of the 1970s, we knew that the photo of the screaming naked girl running from a napalm attack in Vietnam was real, and we didn't want anything like that on our consciences.

My generation has rabbit ears listening for anyone who self-identifies as a victim. This is a reaction based in culture, emotion, ethics, and, yes, practicality: Nobody wants to be in charge of managing a boycott at a major corporation because there is nothing to win and everything to lose. People at huge companies want to be liked by their critics because they were indoctrinated with the ethic that their critics are right.

There is mounting evidence that social concerns are affecting consumer decisions as well as employee recruitment. People simply don't want to go to neighborhood barbecues and be confronted about their contributions to pollution, obesity, and other social ills associated with corporate behavior. It's a lot harder to defend a company when the people in it embrace its critics' agendas.

The collective collapse of will to fight one's critics is now the default position of U.S. and foreign corporations. While some of this is tied to long-term shifts in cultural and generational outlooks, others can be attributed to the pernicious behavior that some enterprises have demonstrated in recent years. The implosion of the financial system, in part due to greed and mismanagement, is not a figment of a neocommunist's imagination. Nor was the BP oil spill in the Gulf of Mexico and the incomprehensible fraud of Bernard Madoff. Nor Lance Armstrong's rampage of deceit.

Still, some scandals are animated less by smoking-gun guilt than they are by the confirmation of a gut-level bias: The privileged George H. W. Bush is out of touch with everyday Americans because he has never seen a supermarket scanner in action; Al Gore is an insufferable smarty-pants because he implied he invented the Internet; Governor Chris Christie is a Jersey-style mafioso who must have messed with a political enemy's bridge traffic as a vendetta; Martha Stewart must have engaged in insider trading because she'd slit your throat if the napkins on her dining room table are misaligned; and Barack Obama is a Muslim because he is biracial, had a Muslim father, and has a name peculiar to American norms.

If a principal triggers a *gut* reaction among relevant audiences that confirms what is being alleged in a controversy, that principal will be more brittle when under attack than one that doesn't elicit such a reaction. "The facts" are collateral to instincts.

The Smiley-Face Culture of Insult

The mindset of companies that emphasize water-treading niceties over service contributes to their risk of drowning when things get rough. Consumers are rightly outraged at the platitude "your call is important to us" when we know it means "my call isn't remotely important to you; only my money is."

Corporations have become mega-corporations, set up to expand, not to serve either their employees or customers. I've been going to the same downtown Washington, D.C., bank for almost thirty years. It has gone through multiple mergers. The people there used to know me as a good small-business customer. I walked in, and they took care of me. Now they don't know me, don't take care of me, and seem actively disinterested in doing so.

I recently went to my bank to make a deposit. I went in when the bank opened, and I was the only customer there. There were three or four executives in glass offices on their computers. There were another four or five people behind the thick glass deposit window. Several more milled about doing indiscernible tasks. Nobody looked at me. When I finally asked for assistance, the woman looked at me as if I had something hanging from my nose.

"Can somebody please help me deposit this check?" I asked.

A bank staffer promptly—and with extreme politeness—began advising me about the bank's new products.

"No products! No niceness!" I pleaded. "Please just deposit my check." I added something like, "Yours is the only bank I've ever encountered where you need a gun to put money *into* it."

Neither my call nor my business is important to my bank. What's important is my money and my prompt departure so that its employees can get back to their smartphones.

Regrettably, these experiences with big businesses are growing more commonplace for most of us. *Buy our stuff, and just get out . . .*

The incapacity of businesses to fulfill their covenants has coincided with a tsunami of corporate courtesies. These palliation campaigns try to instill faith in entities that consumers despise, increasingly with good reason. So what do they do? Commission studies and hold seminars about trust, as if there's a correlation between how many times you incant the word and people ceasing to loathe the behemoths that mistreat them.

Corporate "trust porn" misunderstands the fundamental concept: Trust is earned through sustained, observable behavior, not by engaging in promiscuous displays of self-congratulation about how much a company cares. People trust those that they have reason to believe, not those that are marinating in a mentality that defaults to courtesies over attentiveness.

Even trust earned in the most admirable way possible, through good products, works, and deeds, isn't enough to immunize the reputations of esteemed organizations that find themselves in a riptide of controversy.

Pink Slimed

If ever there was an example of how quickly an inaccurate and disturbing meme as well as a willing media can destroy a business, it is the case of "lean finely textured beef" (LFTB), labeled "pink slime."

LFTB is a low-fat (about 95 percent fat-free) meat product made from 100 percent beef. The producers of LFTB use a minuscule amount of ammonium hydroxide when producing the product to kill bacteria such as E. coli. LFTB is used in products such as hamburgers, meat loaf, and tacos. Its extraordinary success expanded in step with concerns about life-threatening food-borne illnesses in ground beef in the 1980s and 1990s and has been used since the late 1990s. Seventy-three thousand cases of E. coli are reported in the United States each year.

The term "pink slime" metastasized into the broader culture after ABC News referred to LFTB that way 137 times in broadcasts over a four-week period. A mommy blogger at "The Lunch Tray" website, Bettina Siegel, launched a Change.org petition demanding that the U.S. Department of Agriculture forbid the use of LFTB in schools. The petition received 100,000 signatures in four days.

Prior to ABC's coverage, the term "pink slime" had appeared in news articles approximately nine times per year over a two-decade period (1993–2012). In the six months following ABC's coverage, "pink slime" appeared in more than 4,700 news articles. ABC's key reporter on the story, Jim Avila, used Twitter to promote ABC's coverage. #pinkslime soon became a top Twitter trend. A new website created by a food safety activist called stoppinkslime.org went live. In a *Huffington Post* article, petitioner Siegel coined the term "slimewashing."

Beef Products Inc., a producer of LFTB, had been rapidly expanding until the media controversy hit. Consumers became alarmed as a result of the false information being spread about LFTB, as Beef Products alleges in its lawsuit, and longtime customers canceled or scaled back their orders. Public schools in Montgomery County, Maryland, and Fairfax County, Virginia, suburbs of Washington, D.C., confirmed that they would be phasing out LFTB within a few weeks of the ABC broadcast. Beef Products's income dropped from $650 million to $130 million and closed three of its plants, terminating 650 workers. Cargill, which made a product similar to LFTB, suffered an 80 percent volume drop, and another related company filed for bankruptcy protection. Beef Products sued ABC for defamation, seeking $1.2 billion in damages.

Public education, a staple of conventional PR, is a weak antidote to the sheer gross-out factor of "pink slime." It's impossible to answer the vivid and false image of LFTB that Beef Products describes in its complaint with facts alone. Celebrity chef Jamie Oliver inaccurately demonstrated the manufacturing process by dumping a large amount of ammonia—a chemical that, in its most familiar form, is associated with the pungent cleaners used by maintenance crews to mop floors. What Oliver and others failed to show was how a microscopic amount of ammonia hydroxide is actually used when producing the product, and that ammonia is generally recognized as safe by federal regulators and is used with hundreds of products consumed every day.

Largely lost in the debate was the reason that LFTB became such a heavily demanded product in the first place: to provide beef that lowers the risk of food-borne illness. Nancy Donley, who lost her six-year-old son, Alex, to *E. coli*, and who runs the nonprofit group STOP Foodborne Illness, has expressed concern about the "misinformation swirling around the Internet and TV about lean beef produced by Beef Products, Inc." She has also said, "Consumers need to understand that this product is meat, period, and that the use of ammonia hydroxide in minute amounts during processing improves the safety of the product and is routinely used throughout the food industry."

LFTB's alternative products don't have the track record that LFTB has earned over its life span. These alternatives include cheap but highly fatty beef, a product health advocates have been working hard to reduce in the food supply, or expensive lean beef. In all likelihood, school districts with limited budgets will opt for the cheaper, fattier stuff. This will reverse the progress that has been made in recent years on the nutrition front and hinder the prevention of food-borne illnesses, most of which derive from ground beef.

If the objective, however, was a high-profile takedown, the pink-sliming of LFTB was a big success.

Susan G. Komen

Shattering Komen

Established in 1982, Susan G. Komen for the Cure became the most powerful breast cancer charity in the country. Naming it in memory of her sister, who died of the disease, founder Nancy Brinker built an organization that has given about $2 billion to breast cancer research, advocacy, and education since its inception.

The once-unassailable Komen's cultural and political muscle was weakened in a single stroke when the charity announced in early 2012 that it would stop funding the Planned Parenthood Federation of America. Komen had been providing money to Planned Parenthood to conduct breast examinations and mammograms for five years. It focused on patients who didn't have the resources for this checkup through traditional healthcare avenues. This initiative was unrelated to birth control, for which Planned Parenthood is primarily recognized. Komen justified its action by citing a congressional investigation into Planned Parenthood and Komen's rule against funding organizations facing legal or regulatory scrutiny.

The backlash from women's health advocates was immediate and severe. How could Komen, which was known for programs that helped saved women's lives, retreat from something as fundamental as breast cancer detection? The news media, which had supported Komen for decades, turned against the charity. Planned Parenthood raised $400,000 from thousands of donors in short order. Other contributions, including $250,000 from New York mayor Michael Bloomberg, followed.

Despite Komen's position that its decision making wouldn't be political, the term "political" tends to mean "motivated by people we don't like." Allies aren't political; they're just right-thinking. Enemies, however, are political—and mean. Karen Handel, the Komen executive most associated with the original decision to defund Planned Parenthood, was forced out of Komen. She was also a staunch anti-abortion advocate.

On the surface, the decision to defund the breast cancer screenings was unrelated to Planned Parenthood's abortion program. Still, it is hard to imagine that abortion was completely absent from the minds of the players on both sides of this debate, not to mention the media covering it. After all, the initial defunding decision was cheered by religious and pro-life groups and savaged by progressive and women's health groups.

A few days after its ill-fated decision, a shell-shocked Komen reversed it. Nevertheless, participation in Komen's fund-raising events dropped an estimated 15 to 30 percent in 2012, and one of its cornerstone events was reduced from fourteen-city participation to seven cities in 2013. A survey by polling firm Harris Interactive determined that Komen's "brand health" score fell 21 percent from the prior year. In the twenty-three years since Harris began this study, only mortgage lender Fannie Mae suffered a bigger drop, which occurred immediately after the financial crisis in 2009. Brinker announced her retirement from the CEO position a few months after the controversy erupted.

In this chapter, we have seen how the mindsets of besieged principals, the public, and the media contribute to a target's brittleness when attacked. But there is another factor that aggravates this syndrome: the frenzied and misplaced belief in social media as the counteragent to reputational attacks.

> **Takeaway:** Real-world events and a shift in attitudes toward power and victimization have conspired with the modern tools of attack to make the once mighty brittle in the face of attack from parties that were once thought to be weak.

6

Social Media Is the Problem, Rarely the Solution

"But, lo! Men have become the tools of our tools."

HENRY DAVID THOREAU

In September 2013, when a woman of Indian descent, Nina Davuluri, became Miss America, *the top stories* emphasized that some people sent racist tweets about her victory. Wrote the *Washington Post*'s Alexandra Petri, "There's a disturbing trend in news recently where someone's accomplishment is mentioned only in passing but the bulk of the story is dedicated to the fact that Someone Said Something Ignorant About It On Twitter."

Fools have inhabited the earth since the origin of the species, but now the fool's tail wags the cultural dog. There were skeptics at the time of the 1969 moon landing, but the dominant discussion when the *Eagle* landed was about the essential achievement, not the speculation of cranks. Today, however, lunacy, falsehoods, and overreactions reign.

Social Media Idolatry

The scene is becoming so frequent it is now a cliché: A room of anxious middle-aged businesspeople are sitting in a large meeting room listening to a twenty-something person wearing small, rectangular eyewear proselytizing social media. The audience is nodding vociferously, which belies the secret terror many of them are feeling: *I have no idea what this kid is talking about.*

The Anxious Attendees believe that the Social Media Kid seems smart, but they aren't clear about how this "thing" works, how it benefits their business, or how its value is measured. The Anxious Attendees

Brilliant, Innovative CEO Just Wrote Words 'Social Media' On Whiteboard And Underlined It

BOSTON—During this morning's marketing meeting at Dwyer Publishing, Inc., CEO Eric McCulloch astounded and amazed his staff by writing the phrase "Social Media" on a whiteboard in black pen and underlining it. According to sources, McCulloch's virtuoso whiteboard performance has forever rendered traditional advertising pointless and obsolete, and has solved all of Dwyer Publishing's marketing needs in one fell swoop. To the utter astonishment of all in attendance, the veritable titan of industry then pointed at the words "Social Media" on the whiteboard and proclaimed *"this is the future."* "In my entire career, I have never before witnessed with my own two eyes such a dazzling—nay, electrifying—display of cunning insight and business acumen," product manager Jessica Berg told reporters of the visionary and "utterly game-changing" display of word writing and underlining. "The fact that he thought of the words 'Social Media' to begin with is incredibly impressive and forward thinking, but then he actually managed to take it two steps further by not only writing those words in block letters on a whiteboard but—get this—drawing a straight line underneath the words. I mean, the guy's a genius. I guess that's why they pay him the big bucks."

Reprinted with permission of The Onion

know that the Internet is ubiquitous, and indeed they may already enjoy some aspects of it, but something is not clicking. The Social Media Kid seems cool. He's the future. And why do I feel like such a moron?

Not "getting" something cuts two ways. It tells you that you have something to learn, but it also might suggest that the explainer doesn't know quite as much as they seem. The less control and understanding people have, the more they are susceptible to believing in false gods. Enter social media, an important phenomenon, but overrated in its universal application to crisis communication.

When it comes to crisis *creation*, social media is the greatest thing to have come along since magazine television shows; but when it comes to crisis management, social media is of marginal value and often a disaster.

Among my favorite social media backfires:

- In September 2013, an employee at the retailer Rue 21 allegedly told a fourteen-year-old shopper to leave the clothing store because she was "too fat." The young woman, Shelby Buster, went right to Facebook and ignited the Internet. Rue 21 issued a statement online saying it was unable to corroborate the event, which was widely interpreted as calling Buster a liar. The company emphasized that it did "not condone discrimination in any form." Regardless, with social media, in a battle between a retail chain and an earnest fourteen-year-old with a grievance, the young woman wins;

- In late 2013, British Gas attempted to address a 10 percent hike in energy prices by inviting questions from angry consumers on Twitter. The result was sixteen thousand mostly vituperative tweets, many of which included the words "death" and "greed." One asked, "Have you started an affiliate scheme with funeral directors?" referencing an upsurge in the deaths of elderly citizens in the winter months;

- The daughter of departing General Motors CEO Fritz Henderson defended her father on the company's Facebook page with an expletive-laden harangue that referred to his successor as a "SELFISH PIECE OF SHIT" and vowed to never buy from the company again. It was signed "FUCK ALL OF YOU";

- Embattled JPMorgan Chase nixed arrangements to conduct a question-and-answer session on Twitter when the very announcement of the PR strategy was greeted with mocking tweets about the company's recent scandals, including, "What's it like working with Mexican drug cartels? Do they tip?" and "Sorry we ruined your hashtag event, if you could just apologize for your plunder of the global economy, I think we'd be even"; and

- In a promotion sponsored by Durex, the company challenged fans on Facebook to pick a city that should receive a new service called "SOS Condoms," which provides couples with urgent condom delivery. The obscure city of Batman in Turkey defeated Paris and London in the competition, the work of pranksters. Batman is an ultraconservative Muslim city that didn't take kindly to being the subject of a hedonistic Western-style promotion. The result was a gusher of bad news and ridicule.

Social media has ceded vast power to the bathrobe brigade. As Tom Scocca wrote on *Gawker*, "The old systems of prestige are rickety and insecure. Everyone has a publishing platform and no one has a career." Ironically, the bathrobe brigade has far more control over its messages than their conventionally more powerful targets. The Internet is, by its very nature, resistant to any form of command-and-control; however, because we can sit at our laptops, push a button, and see something appear on the screen, we feel a sense of micro-control, dominance over what emanates from our personal domains.

Online advocacy makes the powerless powerful. It allows all of us to be players. A simple scroll through "chat rooms" or the "comments" sections that follow news articles betrays the common denominators of self-appointment and perceived special knowledge. Online, we not only have opinions, we, and only we, know what really happened in Benghazi or Dealey Plaza.

It's not just the bathrobe brigade causing trouble on social media; it is the news media as well. The news media maintain their "old" formats—print, television, and radio—but also have an enormous online presence. In fact, according to the Project for Excellence in Journalism, 20 of the top 25 online news sources are actually the websites of branded "legacy" media outlets such as CNN and the *Washington Post*. Online news is being transmitted faster internationally as well. The British *Daily Mail* boasts the largest online circulation in the world, more than 54 million visitors in January 2013. More than 36 percent of its audience now consists of American readers.

However, many legacy media also use Twitter, Facebook, and other social media outlets to promote their stories and careers. There are a few problems with this. Promoting news on social media erodes the pretense of objectivity. It is advocacy; the news is not being reported in a just-the-facts manner, as it is theoretically supposed to be; it is being hawked. Media outlets promoted their coverage before the Internet, but social media has further commoditized the news, applying greater pressure for it to be sensational and groundbreaking even when it's not.

"Objectivity" is not a legal requirement for the media; it is simply an ethos that emerged during the twentieth century. Still, when journalists merchandise the pretense of objectivity, it becomes harder to uphold this standard against the backdrop of the blatant commercialism of hyping stories on social media.

Context is another problem when social media intersects with news reporting. Social media, by its nature, communicates in staccato bursts of data. It's really just trillions of headlines designed to capture attention. When reporters tweet their coverage, they must summarize it in the most sensational way possible—like a headline. Journalists didn't used to write their stories' headlines. Even if a reporter intends to convey a nuanced portrait of its subject, social media salesmanship makes this a challenge. The chances are that most of the people who see the brief post will never bother to wade into the full news report, leaving the online reader with the impression that the lurid distillation is all they need to know.

Social Media Is Usually Counterproductive in Damage Control

There's lots of water in the world, but you can only drink a small fraction of it. We've got lots of "friends" on Facebook, but we don't know many of them well, and few are actually in our lives. Such is the case with social media and damage control: Lots of it but little that's helpful when things get ugly.

Complicating matters is the etiquette of social media. Removing one's own controversial tweets or Facebook posts is considered bad form. This may seem like a minor violation, but it's taken very seriously in online circles. Online posts are supposed to last forever. Logic would suggest that if a post is offensive, its removal would be desirable. On the digital frontier, transparency demands ongoing offense and, accordingly, keeping the shamed party in an eternal state of mortification. Most vengeance contains the assumption of eternity; a key conception of hell is that every moment brings suffering as intense as the moment that came before. Despite the verbal virtuosity of the transparency ethos, social media is intrinsically at odds with redemption, preferring to remain in crucifixion mode.

In theory, social media encourages dialogue and conflict resolution. When the technology began its emergence, I was hoping this would be the case. However, in practice, social media promotes warfare. Some of this turns on the slippery issue of privacy. Time and again, the most benign communications with hostile parties via social media are treated as a form of trespass. The very act of checking for updates on a critic's website or providing a correction on their Facebook comments section is refracted as a form of espionage. In other words, *How dare you keep abreast of the issue on which we are attacking you?* and *How dare you have the impudence to defend yourself in the same forum where we are impugning you?*

Fact is, most critics don't want to talk; they want to propagandize. This requires that communication flow one way: *I talk. You listen.*

Social media as a phenomenon is staggering in its power, but as a *controllable* defensive narrative device, it is usually ineffective or counterproductive. It builds awareness, but much of what you are trying to do in a crisis is *reduce* awareness. The playbook for inducing sleep is very different from the playbook for generating excitement.

Evangelizing social media assumes that audiences are neutral and want to process unbiased information. In practice, they rarely do, being motivated more by having their existing prejudices confirmed.

Social media conflates "stakeholders" with adversaries. In one of my cases, a large consumer product company we'll call Cleaning Inc. faced outraged customers in the wake of a reformulated-product introduction. Their social media firm advised the company to "engage in dialogue with your stakeholders." What kind of misanthrope wouldn't support that? It has all of the opiates loved by the bien-pensant: Engage. Dialogue. Stakeholders.

Cleaning Inc. proceeded to communicate with its fiercest critics on Facebook and Twitter, which inflamed the critics to the point where they alleged that this huge company was "spying" on them by virtue of their "engagement." Cleaning Inc. had handed over a million megaphones to the bathrobe brigade and paid for it dearly. It aggravated an us-versus-them online debate that migrated to mainstream media outlets.

I have found the case of Cleaning Inc. to be the norm, not the exception, to what happens when big companies attempt to engage outraged consumers via social media. It unleashes unforeseen vitriol. As *Breaking Bad's* Jesse Pinkman warned the Drug Enforcement Administration about tangling with Walter "Heisenberg" White's methamphetamine cartel, "Whatever you think is supposed to happen, the exact reverse opposite is what's gonna happen."

Social media is primarily an offensive technology, a mechanism of attack and building awareness. No one would question that Apple, for example, can publicize new products through social media largely because its customers are already predisposed to be looking for information about the company in this way. Promotion is a different discipline from scandal mitigation. Vindication is, by its nature, deliberative, requiring both storytelling and empathy, which don't fare well with a technology built for speed, anonymity, and unfettered access.

Social Media's Damage Control Function

The most reliable use I have for social media is monitoring what topics are trending relevant to my clients in controversy. I use it as an intelligence-gathering and early-warning tool because what's trending on Twitter or Facebook may suggest where things are—or are not—heading. I use social media to *gather* insight about 90 percent of the time and to disseminate information about 10 percent. I can gauge both the volume and intensity of interest in a particular subject as well as discern the substance of what people think is newsworthy.

I set up "feeds" on a computer screen that monitor a few subjects I'm concerned about. When information scrolls rapidly on my screen, this tells me there is a lot of discussion of an issue. I pay attention. Sometimes there isn't a lot of activity, so I pay less attention.

When there is lots of activity—opinions and articles being shared—I look at content. Is what is being said true? Is it serious? How much do people seem to care? There is an essential difference between chatter and concern, noise and signal.

Monitoring social media can lead to actionable insight. For example, when an activist group boycotted a food client's product, the company panicked. "We must engage our stakeholders," one faction cried. But at my shop, after an initial surge in social media activity, it tapered off, so we counseled against taking major actions. In fact, among the things we saw trending were fans of the product that opposed the boycott.

A few weeks later, a Facebook page that had been established about the boycott had indeed grown in its number of "likes" (or supporters), but we sensed that "liking" the boycott was cheap: People were doing a lot of liking but not much else. There was a lot of superficial activity, but little of it seemed to be converting into action. Again, we were cautious about overresponding. We prepared for an expansion of the boycott, but the campaign evaporated.

Journalist Michael Musto observed that there is "such quick-access media that the scandal stories blow up huge and all-encompassing, then are replaced by the next one three days later." This applies to consumer stories, too. Shortly after, the group that boycotted my client's product moved on to another scourge. This is a quirk of the glass jaw phenomenon: On the one hand, negative information that can cause harm lasts forever on the Internet; on the other hand, just because it's "out there" doesn't mean anybody cares after the initial spark. There is a fine line between correcting defamatory information, which you usually should, and trying to recharacterize disturbing—but not libelous—online posts for posterity, which is trickier because picking a digital scab may infect the wound.

A response to a reputational attack must be anchored in good judgment and with consideration for the consequences of responding, at what speed, in what proportion, and in what duration.

In another of my cases, a client's stock was being hammered on the allegation that the company was misstating its finances. Its CEO was accused of using his wealth and power to bully rivals. The virulence of social media activity in its breadth and falsity of content was so intense that we knew we were in this fight no matter what we did. The executive and his company didn't have many defenders either. We had no fear of provoking a larger controversy because it had *already* expanded. We responded in multiple venues, including putting the CEO on national television, as well as taking legal action for anticompetitive behavior and defamation. Once we made news, we amplified it by linking media appearances, opinion pieces, and legal documents on Facebook, Twitter, and other social media outlets.

The difference in how we advised our clients in the two cases highlighted in this chapter came after serious consideration of the variables at work. In both, we used social media to gauge the state-of-play. In one, we selectively used social media to fight back.

When it comes to technology, all I care about is what it can do. I know that there is something under the hood of my car that's big and hot and black and has hoses and wires, but I could go a thousand lifetimes and never need to spend any time getting to know the engine. As long as my car moves when I turn the key, I'm happy. I get no pleasure tinkering with it and have no need to learn how or why gasoline makes pistons move, or even what a piston looks like.

The same holds true for social media. "Learning" new technologies holds no interest. *Benefiting* from technology does. On Twitter and Facebook, people write a few words about their sentiments and link articles relevant to those sentiments. I understand this and occasionally find it useful. I suspect that many sermonize on social media because they like using it. This is fine until you are managing the reputations and fortunes of others, whereupon there are ethical and strategic considerations about the consequences. Enjoying futzing around on the computer doesn't equate with it serving a strategic or tactical purpose.

Defusing Isolated Incidents

Social media offers opportunities to introduce counterstories into the conversational bloodstream. In crisis management, social media can be effective in: 1) countering demonstrable falsehoods and conveying simple positions and recommended actions, 2) connecting specific audiences to content that carries an alternative narrative to what they may be hearing from adverse parties, and 3) serving as a stalking horse to keep conventional media more honest than they would be otherwise.

When I think about the cases where social media can be useful, I divide crises into two categories: "sniper" and "character." A sniper crisis is episodic, caused by something external or accidental, and is often superficial. Think: The Dominos Pizza employee who was filmed engaging in disgusting behavior in a kitchen where food was being prepared and posted it on YouTube, and when Southwest Airlines kicked off a heavyset passenger who happened to be a movie director with 1.6 million Twitter followers.

A character crisis has at its core an intrinsic flaw or pernicious behavior. Think Enron, BP, or even the meanness associated with charges that New Jersey governor Chris Christie jammed the George Washington Bridge to retaliate against a political intransigent.

Social media lends itself better to tactics associated with sniper crises, which require simple points of information, apologies, corrections, or recommended actions associated with episodic events and customer service updates.

When Southwest Airlines removed indie movie director Kevin Smith in February 2010 because his weight was deemed a "safety risk" to passengers, it tangled with the wrong guy. Smith promptly went on a Twitter rampage about the incident. He queried, "What, was I gonna roll on a fellow passenger?" He later tweeted a photo of himself on a later flight where his weight—which hadn't changed much in a few hours—was apparently not a safety risk. Many of his two hundred tweets were picked up by major media.

Southwest apologized to Smith on Twitter. Smith was offered a voucher for future flights. The company also explained its longstanding policy of requiring "customers of size" to purchase two tickets. Not everybody was impressed, but Southwest earned plaudits for responding. Plenty of people even supported Southwest for reiterating its published policy.

"Fatgate," as it came to be called, receded quickly. Nevertheless, at the time Southwest responded, the Twitter war was already in full swing. Inflaming the controversy wasn't really a factor because it had already been inflamed. Southwest's apology, voucher grant, and reiteration of its policy were straightforward. They were in and out.

Similarly, in the aftermath of the repulsive video featuring a Domino's employee defiling food, the company responded both on Twitter, where the video had been circulated, and with a message from its CEO on YouTube, where it had originally aired. Both venues emphasized the specific actions the company takes to ensure customer safety and product integrity. Again, straightforward.

In neither the Southwest nor Domino's events, however, was there a suggestion that a dangerous form of behavior had been institutionalized at these companies. While there are plenty of people concerned about the treatment of overweight passengers, there are also many who privately supported Southwest's long-established policy. And even though the behavior of the Domino's employee was revolting, the company wasn't encouraging this practice. These indisputable factors helped medicate an online problem with an online treatment.

As we saw earlier with the Rue 21, British Gas, and JPMorgan Chase examples, managing character crises on social media often backfires because emotions are running high and adversaries, not to mention the universe of social media users, tend to treat communications as acts of war. There is a feeling that greater powers are trying to spin their way out of a complicated mess by invading the rest of our computers with glib messaging. When an event is seen to have been isolated, however, audiences are more receptive to social media venues.

Social media is both a powerful phenomenon and a cliché for technological panaceas. Next we will look at some of the strategic clichés that are invoked in many discussions of scandal management.

> **Takeaway:** When it comes to managing controversy, social media carries more risks than benefits and should be handled with care.

WHO DO YOU THINK YOU'RE SPINNING?

7

The Eight Most Baseless Crisis Management Clichés

"Models work when they are appropriate for the particular circumstance, but some of the best investment judgments over time have come when people recognized that models derived in other periods were broken or not directly relevant."

—ABBY JOSEPH COHEN

So far, we have seen how glass-jawed principals are everywhere and have a sense of why they are so vulnerable. As much trouble as our proverbial boxer is in, however, the fight doctors aren't very effective either. Damage control has rapidly become defined by parasitic clichés—easy-to-digest chestnuts that sound so reasonable and have been repeated so often that they have infected most discussions of controversies as if they were demonstrated cures. To participate in a corporate strategy meeting is to bear witness to magical thinking whereby regurgitation of these bromides is a proxy for making them happen.

This chapter will explore eight of the most overused clichés.

CLICHÉ #1: *"Get Ahead of the Story"*

Perhaps the most virulent of the clichés surrounding reputational issues is the insipid "get ahead of the story," a concept which suggests that a deft maneuver or two could have prevented the controversy. The next time a major controversy hits and you decide to subject yourself to the Fiasco Vortex, watch how long it takes for a crisis expert to trot out this beauty.

"Get ahead of the story" is the equivalent of telling a cardiac patient in the emergency room, "Don't have a heart attack." Maintaining a good diet, taking appropriate medications, and exercising contribute to good cardiovascular health. Similarly, making good products and avoiding bad behavior will reduce the chances of becoming embroiled in controversy. Nevertheless, by the time a crisis hits, the virus has already been introduced into the system.

In the era prior to the Fiasco Vortex, it was easier to prevent many controversies by making adverse parties sign confidentiality agreements in exchange for money or by modifying a questionable product before its flaws went metastatic.

But how do you get ahead of something that moves at the speed of light? When I get most cases, the catalyst has already occurred, and "getting ahead" of it is no longer an option.

During the Tiger Woods scandal, I did a few interviews about the case.* On one television interview, I was paired with a sports reporter who recommended that Tiger "get ahead of the story," adding, "all of these women kept crawling out of the woodwork to discuss their alleged liaisons with Tiger."

I said (paraphrasing from memory), "I know women are crawling out of the woodwork. How does Tiger get 'ahead' of that?"

---

* When I became involved with one of Woods's corporate sponsors, I ceased doing news analysis.

The reporter repeated that as long as women keep coming forward, this story wouldn't die. "He should have gotten ahead of it."

Without trying to be a complete jerk, I again asked, *"How?* Should he hire assassins to track down every Hooters waitress in the country and shoot her before she hires Gloria Allred?"

There was some laughter. No, that wouldn't be a good idea, we agreed.

"Okay," I continued. "Should he have held a press conference days before the car accident that ignited this cascade and said, 'Hey, everybody, one of these days I may get into a car accident because my wife may get mad at me after she reads my texts from other women, and I want to give everybody a heads-up so that if this happens, everybody'll lighten up on me. Cool?' "

More laughter.

I explained that I dwell in the world of the brutally practical. I'm not hired to theorize. I saw no way, in accordance with the laws of the universe, that Tiger could have gotten ahead of this story once he had made the decision to serially have affairs and maintain extensive electronic documentation of them.

Other pundits suggested that Tiger should have paid all of the women to keep quiet. This approach had some merit in yesteryear but is harder these days. For one thing, paying out (perfectly lawful) hush money would have required tremendous foresight on Tiger's part. For another, we were talking about more than one indiscretion here. Multiple parties make such a damage control strategy a very leaky vessel. I wouldn't be surprised if some of the women involved with this scandal were compensated for signing "gag orders," but that others were sufficiently angry and publicity-hungry that they preferred the media attention. People who become involved with scandals are rarely the types who hold covenants dear or think through the consequences of their actions.

Finally, there is a dangerous assumption at the root of "get ahead of the story," which is that the act of disclosure will be greeted with prim appreciation as opposed to being used as a weapon against the principal. When you are up against motivated adversaries who have no incentive to preserve a positive relationship with you, you have to consider how they will respond as opposed to how you would like them to respond given what's at stake.

The next time you hear someone recommend getting ahead of the story, ask them *how*, and play out each scenario associated with that recommendation with respect to human nature and the Fiasco Vortex.

CLICHÉ #2: *"Respond Immediately"*

A derivative of "get ahead of the story" is the call to "respond immediately." This is a well-intended recommendation that had its origins in a time when "immediately" translated into "before a reporter's deadline." This usually meant around 4 p.m., when a newspaper "went to bed" and nightly news broadcasts were "in the can." If you missed those deadlines, it was unlikely that your point of view would be reflected in the coverage. Responding within these times frames was easy; it was self-interest and common courtesy.

Today, deadlines barely exist because the news never goes to bed. Moreover, immediate and full responses can be tricky because crisis principals are either focusing on triage—prioritizing needs— or may not know the relevant facts.

When the NASDAQ blew a fuse and went dark in August 2013, a reporter asked me what I thought about the exchange's "mismanagement" of the glitch because the CEO hadn't called her back to do an on-air interview.

"It's not about *you!*" I told her. She was a sport about it, and I explained that the CEO, Robert Greifeld, was surely focusing on getting the exchange back up and running, as he should have been.

In a perfect world, he would have made a media appearance, but the immediate operational issue trumped public relations.

Think of a pilot whose airplane encounters turbulence. His passengers need assurances as soon as possible, but his instincts and training are rightly telling him to address the physics and mechanics of the situation first. Keeping the plane in the air is what has to be done *immediately*.

The logical, but misplaced, demand to respond immediately has sometimes pressured principals to make claims before they know the relevant facts. BP was criticized for not making accurate projections about the quantity of oil flowing into the Gulf of Mexico, as if the company was being willfully deceptive. The truth was that the government's flow rate projections were equally inaccurate, coming in at about 1,000 barrels per day as opposed to the estimate of 5,000 barrels that was eventually determined. As a BP spokesperson said in eloquent simplicity, "There's just no way to measure it." BP had emphasized on several occasions that its main task was "stopping the leak, not measuring it," summarized the *New York Times*.

After the 2001 anthrax attacks, the U.S. Postal Service rapidly made assurances that the mail supply was safe—before it knew whether this were true. In the days that followed, two postal workers died from anthrax intoxication at the very same Washington, D.C., facility from which these assurances were given.

In 2007, after massive recalls of pet food, one manufacturer took out advertisements touting that its own ingredients were in the clear. Shortly afterward, the company, Blue Buffalo, recalled one-third of its product line, according to *USA Today*. It turned out that some of its sourcing material came from China, then a poorly regulated market, which had also been the provenance of the contamination that had sparked the recall.

These examples beg the question: Is it better to respond immediately before you know what's happening in order to be responsive

U.S. Post Office linked to Anthrax deaths

to the media's demands or wait until you have your facts straight to offer specific assurances? The answer depends on a variety of factors, but given that no matter what you do, it will be declared "too little too late," I prefer to take a breath before responding too quickly.

In high-stakes situations, we rarely know much immediately. The first version you hear about a troubled figure will not be the same version that you hear as the crisis runs its course. Occasionally, the principal is lying or stonewalling. Other times, the explanation may simply be psychic denial or incomplete information. Either way, running with an early version of events is risky.

One of the bigger mistakes of my early career comes to mind. In the 1980s, a client that had been accused of environmental violations had assured me that a particular operational problem had been corrected. I, in turn, had conveyed this to a local reporter, on deadline, who ran with it. As it turned out, the problem had not yet been fully corrected and I looked like an idiot at best, a liar at worst. To this day, I don't know if I had been deliberately misled by my client or if there had been a miscommunication somewhere in the process. What I do know is that in my youthful zeal to impress a client, I hadn't pressed hard enough for the truth and hurt my credibility in the process.

Crises don't unfold in a linear manner. We never know what reactions will be triggered when a catalyst occurs. One of the perverse benefits of the Fiasco Vortex is that sometimes a potential scandal gets lost in the noise. I had a client caught up in the subprime meltdown that was contemplating a big PR counterstrike at around the time the Bernard Madoff Ponzi scheme broke. The media that were following our case were diverted to Madoff. We let them enjoy their diversion as my true objective was getting my client out of the vortex in order to plan a more thoughtful defense. Our client was not sympathetic in the context of the times, but he and his company were not on the same exponent as Madoff. By counting a beat, we achieved a lot more than if we had acted immediately.

The prevailing wisdom on consumer safety issues is that companies should recall their products immediately upon hearing of an adverse report. The problem with this is that manufacturers would be recalling products all day, every day, if they heeded this advice, because they receive adverse reports constantly.

The ethic of immediacy was memorialized in the film *The Insider,* about the tobacco industry whistle-blower Jeffrey Wigand. The film falsely asserted that Johnson & Johnson (J&J) "instantly" recalled Tylenol in 1982 when the company heard there had been tampering with its capsules. It actually took J&J a week to recall the product, which only happened after retailers such as CVS and Walgreen's pulled the product from their shelves after the first death was reported.

Not only is it a myth that J&J recalled Tylenol instantly; the company could not have done so because it wasn't *instantly* evident that its products were the problem. It wasn't until several days into the tragedy, when the authorities and the company realized that two people in the same family who had used Tylenol from the same package had died, that the linkage could be made.

The most responsible way to evaluate the need for immediate action is to consider the veracity and seriousness of what is being alleged. Once J&J realized that there were credible reports of people dying, Tylenol was recalled. What else was J&J going to do? Keep a lethally compromised product on the shelves? Of course not, but it's important to keep in mind the difference between verifiable reports of fatalities and the over-the-transom noise that operations hear about regularly.

In *The Insider, 60 Minutes* reporter Mike Wallace (played by Christopher Plummer) asks producer Lowell Bergman (played by Al Pacino) why the traumatized whistle-blower Jeffrey Wigand and his family are so unpredictable when it comes to making a decision about his appearance on the program. Bergman/Pacino answers, "Ordinary people under extraordinary pressure, Mike. What the hell do you expect, grace and consistency?"

CLICHÉ #3: *"Come Clean"*

Sometimes scandal principals mistake a therapeutic action for a strategic one. One of the most powerful human urges when faced with scandal is to talk, and talk a lot. Verbal diarrhea is always self-exculpatory and involves a lot of denial. Stream-of-consciousness expression is inevitably fraught with half-truths, untruths, and self-incrimination.

The "get it all out there" ethos is quaint advice from another time. It is the equivalent of the medieval practice of "bleeding" patients who were sick, the logic being that the toxins or evil spirits would be released from their system.

The cry to "come clean" underpinned coverage surrounding Martha Stewart's insider trading scandal. The problem was that her legal position was that she was not guilty. She could not come clean knowing that her attorneys were seeking her acquittal on the grounds that she hadn't committed a crime. If she had confessed, it would have signaled an entirely different legal strategy. Besides, in the end, it wasn't insider trading that convicted Martha Stewart; it was lying to the authorities. In other words: *Talking*. *in a Depo? If so, what choice did she have?*

The big problem with the hyper-application of coming clean is that it assumes universal guilt. Plenty of people and institutions accused of crimes and other infractions didn't commit them.

Reporters notoriously abet the confessional ethic with the oft-repeated swindle that if the target just comes clean or, in today's parlance, is "transparent," that will be best. Best for whom? Best for the reporter, that's who.

Joan Didion put it well: "My only advantage as a reporter is that I am so physically small, so temperamentally unobtrusive, and so neurotically inarticulate that people tend to forget that my presence runs counter to their best interests. And it always does. That is one last thing to remember: writers are always selling somebody out."

If immediate disclosure and a passion for transparency truly are scandal cures, why do the news media, when faced with their own messes, stonewall, dissemble, defend their practices, hide behind lawyers, and lash out at their accusers? The answer is some combination of human nature and pragmatism. When media executives find themselves in crisis, they rapidly determine that there aren't easy answers, and may not be answers at all.

Having advised media companies under siege, I have seen two polarizing instincts at work. First is the impulse that all targets of attack feel: the desire to neutralize their accusers. Second is the recognition that the integrity of their organization is at stake and that a blue-ribbon-style self-examination may be the only option.

But getting news organizations to this point is a tough slog because of the narcissistic wound of being the accused.

Being an accuser is a lot more fun. You get to feel a sense of righteousness while doing your job, a self-perception of our jobs that few of us have. Then there is the narcotic rush of pulling a trigger and watching big game in the distant trajectory of a barrel go down.

When reporters argue that confession is the best strategy, what they are really saying is that confessions are good for *us, the press.* And they are: Confessions make superb copy.

Confessions can help a principal disarm a controversy, but they should be considered a very specific course of treatment to be used only if certain requirements are met. Among those requirements are legal (Will it get the principal into trouble?), veracity (Did the principal actually do anything wrong?), capability (Is the principal capable of executing a confession?), news congestion (What else is happening that can affect the tactic?), and efficacy (Is it likely to work?).

The confessional drive is further abetted by the impression many otherwise sophisticated principals hold that they have some kind of quasi-legal obligation to journalists, as if profit-seeking media enterprises carry the force of a subpoena. They don't. The media's power isn't judicial, it's reputational: Industrial-scale distributors of information can destroy lives, institutions, and careers, deservedly or not. Communicating with the media should be based on cold self-interest. Those for whom public opinion has strategic importance often must interact with the press in dicey situations, but the terms of communication can be negotiated.

Transparency is not a synonym for "we're nice people"; it's a strategy of full disclosure. It means taking an inventory of your affairs and making them public, which is a fine touchstone but not always doable. I have been in countless meetings where transparency is cited as a core value. Then I ask, "Do you really intend to disclose everything that your critics want disclosed?" The answer is usually some form of "Well, we can't."

There are consequences of full disclosure—legally, strategically, security-wise, and to competitors. At the moment, everybody high-fives when they invoke transparency, but sooner or later, somebody's going to demand to see your cards and isn't going to be pleased when you won't show them.

It's also important to consider the extent to which your adversaries are being transparent. Hint: They're probably not.

Those who demand transparency are sometimes the least likely to be able to practice it. I spoke to a reporter on a client's behalf who demanded an open-ended interview with the corporate CEO to question him about allegations the reporter was being fed by a whistle-blower. I demurred because it sounded like an ambush, and I didn't want my client providing play-by-play commentary when we didn't fully understand the implications. My discomfort was poorly received. "You're not being transparent," the reporter said.

"Who are your sources?" I asked.

"You know I can't tell you that," the reporter said.

"Well, you're not being very transparent," I said.

I didn't expect the reporter would reveal his sources, but I was making a point that in this context transparency didn't mean transparency: It meant, *I want dirt to use against your client*, which is not the same thing. We ended up responding with detailed written documentation.

The targets of transparency campaigns are always the same: big business and government. That's fine, but where is the call for greater scrutiny of crisis creators, including NGOs, short sellers, plaintiffs' lawyers, and major media? There are neither appetites nor budgets for such pursuits. After all, a call for hard-nosed scrutiny of perceived vindicators is viewed as being Orwellian. By seizing the rhetoric and symbolism of transparency, its proponents have rendered themselves immune from that which they champion. Let's call "transparency," as it is practiced, what it is: opposition research.

The media play an important watchdog role in keeping a check on power, but not all targets are the Nixon White House or Bernie Madoff. Targets need not abet their own downfalls or, even worse, delude themselves into believing that they will be rewarded for self-incrimination.

Not everything lends itself to perfect transparency. Would the world have been better served seeing a young Franklin Delano Roosevelt howling in pain as he crawled along the floor futilely trying to overcome polio. Or known about Abraham Lincoln's and Winston Churchill's crippling depressions? Do we really want undercover cops or national security operatives posting their identities on a website?

Coming clean has theoretical virtues and practical limitations. Damage control is not like psychotherapy or religious confession, where recognition of a problem leads to a catharsis and, ultimately, adaptive behavior. Psychotherapy and religious confession happen in private for a reason: Before you can get right with the world, you have to get right with yourself.

CLICHÉ #4: *"We've Got to Tell Our Side of the Story"*

The first seed of modern crisis management was planted during Watergate. The great counterfactual canard that has been repeated countless times is that if Nixon had just admitted everything right away and said, "I screwed up," the whole thing would have fizzled out. No, he would have been run out of Washington within days given the operating environment and the nature of the sins. Once Nixon had embarked on his doomed journey, there was no life raft for him.

There is no playbook about when to speak and when to remain silent other than that the key variable is the *probable* benefit to the principal. If you have a good counternarrative, this recommends saying more. A weaker defense recommends silence. Either way, sitting down with the press is a tactic, not a strategy. The key questions are *To what end are you meeting?* and *What exactly are you going to say at this meeting?*

You can only tell your side of the story when you *have* a side of the story. Preferably something other than, "We totally did all of those illegal things you're alleging—and you don't even know the half of it!"

There are casualties of the "just ask me anything" ploy. *Fortune* magazine's Bethany McLean is widely credited with being a driving force behind the exposing of fraud at Enron. In early 2001, McLean hypothesized that she was onto serious accounting irregularities at Enron. After extensive reporting, McLean asked for greater explication on certain items prior to publication. Enron obliged by flying high-ranking executives, including chief financial officer Andrew Fastow, to meet with *Fortune*. In a two-hour meeting, Fastow performed an opera of legerdemain. Among his tactics was to insist that he could not reveal the name of the key executive at a questionable unit within the company because it was confidential. It turned out that the name of this executive had been published in Enron's proxy statement two years earlier. It was Fastow himself.

Fortune's story about Enron ran in February 2001 and served as the proverbial bat to the hornet's nest. "How exactly does Enron make its money?" a credit analyst at Standard & Poor's asked in the piece. "If you figure it out, let me know." Fastow's dissembling and doubletalk didn't deter McLean, *Fortune*, or the Justice Department. Enron collapsed in November 2001.

Would Enron have been spared had it not sat down with *Fortune*? No, but the company wouldn't have accelerated its demise through a misplaced devotion to spin. Plenty of targets that didn't try to spin the press were either spared as a result of their discretion or took a lesser hit.

A similar principle applies to the ambush that the attorney for Yankees legend Alex Rodriguez endured on the *Today* show when he went on to address his client's alleged use of performance-enhancing drugs. Joe Tacopina, A-Rod's lawyer, announced he had "so many things I'd like to say." Interviewer Matt Lauer presented him with a waiver from Major League Baseball that would permit him to discuss A-Rod's history with performance-enhancing drugs. Nevertheless, Tacopina persisted with the mantra that there were many things he'd "love" to say, but he didn't say anything, which only inflamed the controversy.

As a lawyer, Tacopina was probably right in not engaging in on-the-fly commentary. But what objective had been met by doing the *Today* interview at all? In theory, the objective was probably to put pressure on Yankee management for their landmark 211-game suspension of A-Rod for doping. A live interview, however, isn't theory: It's *theater* designed to stone a cultural witch. Force of personality alone won't beat back the one-two punch to the jaw in the form of Matt Lauer and a signed waiver.

Someone else who didn't think media engagement through was Congressman Anthony Weiner when he was confronted with allegations of tweeting photos of his nether regions in 2011. His first instinct was to do what was familiar, not what was smart: hold an impromptu news conference and leverage his confidence to start bullshitting. The result was a masterpiece in self-immolation because his guilt in this affair was absolute, provable, and nonnegotiable.

In contrast, Tiger Woods was roundly pilloried for not telling his side of the story immediately after his infamous 2009 car accident. Weiner was wrong to talk; Tiger was right to clam up because he didn't *have* a very good side of the story. There were potential

New York 1

legal issues at stake (domestic and vehicular), and he didn't want to incriminate himself and his wife. There were also things to work out with his sponsors and his wife that took precedence over his obligations to reporters. Besides, Tiger Woods is a golfer, not a Clintonian scandal maestro facile in the improvisational arts.

In almost every case I have ever worked on, the client believed she had a good story to tell. This is a wish, not a strategy. Many in the media only want to hear your side of the story to boost ratings and win awards at your expense. Another problem is that your side of the story may be terrible.

Plenty of controversial figures have engaged in *sitzfleish* (German for sitting on one's rear), riding out a storm. Pivoting and counterpunching may play a role, but the modus operandi here is simple endurance. Endurance is the most unheralded brand of genius. Johnny Carson's career, Bill and Hillary Clinton's ability to stay in the game, Ronald Reagan's assumption of the presidency at almost seventy, the productivity of Woody Allen and Joyce Carol Oates are endless sources of awe. Nevertheless, the longevity of each can be traced to their exercise of their core talents, not spin.

A core fallacy of the "tell your story" cliché is the idea that tactics that worked well for one principal will work for others. Fans of quarterback-without-a-home Tim Tebow learned about the limits of public relations stunts when in September 2013 they tried to hold a rally to pressure the Jacksonville Jaguars to sign him. The rally attracted... eleven Tebow fans, somewhat short of the threshold that would make the Jaguars' front office recruit Tebow. The sad little rally received more coverage *as a joke*, surely not the organizers' intentions. NBC Sports wrote, "We predicted the event, which was scheduled to begin at 3:16 p.m. ET on Monday and due to last three hours and 16 minutes, would draw between three and 16 people. It looks like it did."

Believing that good PR tactics are transferrable and replicable is kind of like frumpy comedian Louis C.K. saying, *Brad Pitt looked good shirtless in* Thelma & Louise, *so I'll go shirtless in my comedy tour in order to become a sex symbol.* Extraordinary communications campaigns are only effective if they intersect with extraordinary messengers during extraordinary times. Everybody with an offensive or defensive proposition wants it to "go viral." If it were simply a matter of deploying the right tactics, everything would go viral, and everybody would be elected president or create the iPad. As Joan Cusack's character said in the film *Working Girl* (with a nasal Staten Island accent), "Sometimes I sing and dance around the house in my underwear. Doesn't make me Madonna. Never will."

CLICHÉ #5: *Speak with One Voice*

Toward the beginning of my career, I worked for a firm that had the phrase "Speak with one voice" as a motto. It appeared in some of their promotional literature and was often a point of counsel to clients facing communications challenges. As the years passed, I came to realize that it was also the motto for a lot of other outfits, too. It's still used today.

Speaking with one voice sounds smart in its singleness of purpose and consistency. After all, who would adopt a motto such as "Send mixed messages"? Marketing campaigns benefit from such clarity, but this doesn't always transfer to managing controversies.

Many besieged organizations have a fetish for consistency. Scandal principals should be consistent in their *direct* rhetoric, but not necessarily in their comprehensive approach to crisis management. On the day he was impeached, Bill Clinton's throaty voice incanted, "We must stop the politics of personal destruction." What he was really saying was, "We must stop the politics of personal destruction as it pertains to *me*, not to my enemies." The subtext was, "Take these bastards out, would you?"

Clinton was savvy enough to realize that the concept of speaking with one voice was no way for a president to fight a multi-front war. Not only were multiple voices necessary to survive this scandal, but Clinton had multiple supporters with platforms.

One of them was *Hustler* magazine publisher, Larry Flynt, who was outraged by hypocritical Republicans attacking Clinton for the same types of extramarital adventures that they were also having. With the help of investigative journalist Dan Moldea, Flynt's efforts exposed the dalliances of key Republican members of Congress who were hostile to Clinton. While not directed by the White House, this effort played a pivotal role in saving Clinton's presidency because it showed the public that the president's critics were not materially different from him. This dissuaded certain public officials from taking the crusade against Clinton too far, lest their own nocturnal explorations be exposed.

Mobilizing surrogates with different messages can be preferable to rigid adherence to speaking with one voice.

CLICHÉ #6: *A Crisis Is an Opportunity*

The only people who believe that a crisis is an opportunity are those who either have never been through one or have had the good fortune to survive. Crises seriously damage individuals and organizations. Some never recover. The survivors get to write history accompanied by self-serving reflections that attribute success to the superior leadership of those in charge. Sometimes the survivors deserve praise for their skills, and much can be learned from them, but many besieged principals make the best decisions they can under the circumstances and are still defeated.

What doesn't kill you may make you stronger, but that's only if it doesn't kill you. If anything, a crisis is an opportunity for someone *else*, not the principal.

The infrequency with which crises truly become opportunities doesn't mean that there isn't hope for surviving a controversy. There are many survivors of reputational crises, including sportscaster Marv Albert, who went on trial for sexual assault in the 1990s and, after being convicted of a lesser charge, reemerged in broadcasting a few years later. But it doesn't mean that principals long for the days of their near destruction.

CLICHÉ #7: *Change the Conversation*

In an episode of *Mad Men*, advertising ace Don Draper impressed a prospective client that was concerned about their stale image when he remarked, "If you don't like what's being said, change the conversation." This is actually an old trope, one that has been bandied about in crisis war rooms for decades, and it's always received as a revelation.

Everybody under siege wants to change the conversation. I'm

sure when the oil rig in the Gulf of Mexico blew up, BP wished it could say, *"How about those rascals at Goldman Sachs? We need congressional hearings—NOW!"*

The reality is that the conversation can only be changed when there is something else that people want to talk about. In 2005, when a human finger turned up in a cup of Wendy's chili, the conversation didn't change until a month later, when the authorities identified a suspect who had placed the severed digit in the chili as part of a shakedown scheme. Only then did the conversation change from being about bad food service to being about crime.

For years, Lance Armstrong was able to change the conversation away from alleged doping by putting the blame on external parties like cutthroat French officials jealous of his predominance. Attacking a cancer survivor, no less! But by early 2013, the jig was up; Armstrong was a serial cheat, so what else was there to talk about?

The Bush administration was successful in changing the conversation from al-Qaeda to Saddam Hussein, even though the latter was not involved with the 9/11 attacks. Given Saddam's track record of using chemical weapons against his own people, it was entirely plausible that he had been stockpiling weapons of mass destruction (WMDs). Accordingly, Bush had a justification for invading Iraq that he probably really believed in. When no WMDs were discovered, however, the Bush machine that was supposedly filled with mind-control wizards failed to come up with an alternative to the reigning narrative, "Bush lied, people died."

You can only change the conversation when the alternative narrative is plausible and resonant.

CLICHÉ #8: *"Educate Our Stakeholders"*

The term "stakeholders" has infested the lexicon of corporations and institutions. Big outfits have stakeholders, but in controversies they also have motivated adversaries. This is a very distressing concept to bureaucrats who are hardwired for conflict avoidance. An executive under siege from a powerful NGO once asked me to nix references to "adversaries" from a presentation.

"Why?" I asked.

"We don't have adversaries," the executive said.

"What do you have?"

"We have stakeholders," he said.

"When John Wilkes Booth showed up at Ford's Theatre, was he a stakeholder?" I asked. When the exec went pale, I explained that an NGO had explicitly stated its aim to put his company out of business. "If I can't call them what they are, I'd be giving a deliberately false diagnosis, and I'm not going to do that."

Those who survive controversies tend to have constituencies. Somebody *wants* them to survive. Bill Clinton survived the Lewinsky drama in large measure because the cohort most likely to be offended by his behavior, women, largely supported him. Clinton's handlers may have exploited this sentiment, but they didn't invent it. Many women liked Clinton because of his personal charm and political agenda, which included a progressive position on abortion and women's rights.

Not everyone who faces a crisis has stakeholders or constituents. Plus, who says these audiences *want* to be educated? The public is more like a petulant teenager who is actively hostile to parental input, not a discerning graduate student who took out loans to get an education and is motivated to listen. It is the height of arrogance for attack targets to believe that others are blank slates longing to be enlightened by the wisdom of those they distrust.

As pleasing as it may be to think that human beings routinely determine their worldviews by processing information, a widening body of evidence suggests that preexisting biases determine the facts we choose to believe. A Yale study demonstrated that political biases might go as far as to affect a person's ability to do arithmetic. The research found that respondents with a strong aptitude for math failed to solve problems if they believed the answer would contradict their core beliefs.

For example, if a respondent was told that the answer to the question concerned a "law banning private citizens from carrying concealed handguns in public," they were more likely to flub the answer if they supported gun rights (as opposed to if they thought that the answer involved a relatively neutral subject like skin cream). Interestingly, at both ends of the political spectrum, the more facile respondents were with numbers, the *more* they let their political biases bollix their calculations.

Informing the public can be helpful in managing controversies when there is a clear and powerful counterstory, or when specific actions are being prescribed for audiences with a natural investment in the issue at hand, such as in the recall of a product that they own.

When several young men were wrongly identified as the Boston Marathon bombers, the capture of the guilty Tsarnaev brothers ended the speculation about the innocents. The blatant falsity of the initial rumors defused the allegations.

When a product is being recalled, and an auto company communicates with its customers about which products are affected and tells them precisely what they should do to implement repairs, "education" can be very effective. Both the bombing suspects and recall examples represent specific conditions where the imparting of information mitigated the controversy. Absent these conditions, "education" can be a long slog.

Even if a principal succeeds in educating adverse parties and blank slates, what then? It is not in the interest of critics to stop criticizing. While defusing tensions through "dialogue" is sometimes possible, it often assumes that the core problem is a misunderstanding. An exasperated client once bemoaned her failure to quell hostilities with a consumer advocate after her company demonstrated its new safety procedures to the advocate in a tour of their plant. The advocate kept up her attack despite the plant tour. I assured my client that while her firm's safety demonstration was well intentioned, it did nothing to cure the advocate's desire for fame, which was really driving this affair. Score: Publicity-1; Earnestness-0.

Crisis Cliché Bingo			
"Transparency"	"Get ahead of the story"	"A crisis is an opportunity"	"Speak with one voice"
"Respond immediately"	"Come clean / Get it all out there"	"Dialogue"	"Apologize"
"Change the conversation"	"Trust"	"If you're in a hole, stop digging"	"Engage with our stakeholders"
"Tell our side of the story"	"Corporate social responsibility"	"Tylenol"	"Stay on message"

In addition to the clichés analyzed here, there is another overapplied controversy bromide in need of deconstruction: the apology, which we will now examine.

> **Takeaway:** Damage control clichés are comforting, but they have little grounding in demonstrable, real-world effectiveness. Some are desirable touchstones, but their practical consequences need to be thought out before being applied.

8

The Three Apologies

"But wilt thou know, O vain man, that faith without works is dead?"

—JAMES 2:20

When scandal figures do wrong—and even when they don't—an apology is often the price of admission in a program of repentance. The besieged, however, tend to view apologies as marking the end of the process and are often disappointed when apologizing doesn't defuse the controversy. Redemption takes time, especially given variables such as the nature of the sin, the truth of the allegations, and the power of the principal's constituency.

Apologies come in different types and serve different purposes. They fall into three main categories, which I think of as: the Judeo-Christian Apology, the Transactional Apology, and the "Marital" Apology.

The Judeo-Christian Apology

The Judeo-Christian Apology captures the original objective of forgiveness: to "get right" with God, and to repair the damage done to those who were injured by one's actions. True repentance is the aim, and pain is the price. The supplicant admits to, and genuinely regrets, his choices and mistakes. He is punished and then takes tangible actions to repent. Judeo-Christian Apologies don't anticipate drive-through forgiveness. Suffering is assumed, and no party favor is sought in exchange.

Examples of contemporary Judeo-Christian Apologies are those of financier Michael Milken, who went to prison after being convicted of securities fraud in 1989, and Charles Colson, who was incarcerated for crimes associated with the Watergate scandal.

Milken has dedicated his post–Wall Street life and enormous wealth to issues such as prostate cancer research (a disease from which he suffers), medical research for other life-threatening diseases such as skin cancer and epilepsy, higher education, financial aid, teaching, nutrition, and opportunities for minority youth.

Milken didn't undertake these initiatives solely as part of a PR program designed to burnish his image. He had, in fact, been supportive of many of these causes before he found himself in trouble. While it's impossible to read his mind, Milken's supporters contend (as do I) that he both believed in these causes and recognized that winning quick plaudits was not the true objective. Having gone to prison and been banned from the securities industry for life, it wasn't as if there were tactical objectives to be met. Milken wanted to occupy the rest of his life with good works and undoubtedly hoped that a by-product of these efforts would yield redemption.

Years after Watergate, Charles Colson said, "I went to prison, voluntarily. I deserved it." No equivocating or prevaricating. When he emerged from prison, Colson said he would devote the remainder of his life to his Christian faith, and he did. He created the Prison Fellowship Ministries for inmates and the Justice Fellowship, a faith-based justice reform group. When he won the $1 million Templeton

Prize for Progress in Religion, he gave all of the money to the Fellowship Ministries.

Colson was one of the modern originators of convicts "finding God." Some roll their eyes when bad guys start preaching the gospel. Nevertheless, when Colson's post-Watergate life is examined, and the depth of his devotion and works are appreciated, it's hard to argue that his religious awakening was a short-term gambit to achieve some earthly reward.

After giving a speech where I had praised Milken's work, a questioner took issue with my characterization of Milken as having redeemed himself. "I'll never forget his conviction for manipulating the markets," the questioner said.

I defended my position: The goal of redemption is not, and never has been, to get people to unremember misdeeds. Colson's good works did not delete the word "Watergate" from his 2012 obituary. The true aim is to atone for one's sins, to pay its price, and, in the spiritual sense, return to God's grace in the Judeo-Christian sense. Redemption is not a public relations bullet point. It is not a line item on a marketing proposal to be checked, and whatever deity or interlocutor came up with the concept knew this; otherwise redemption wouldn't really be redemption. It would be a worthless token deposited into a toll basket.

Yet, this is what many contemporary scandal figures want—to essentially be *rewarded* for sins in the form of instant forgiveness. This is the opposite of penance.

Moreover, on a tactical level, with the advent of the Internet, which is infinite and permanent, unremembering is an even more implausible objective than it had once been. The days of scoundrels like Joseph Pulitzer and Cecil Rhodes being able to burnish their names in a generation or two have passed. If you're not sure why these creators of the famous prizes that bear their names were scoundrels, Google them.

Most individuals and institutions in crisis want their apologies to be recognized as Judeo-Christian in nature, when they are, in fact, a form of tactical apology that I'll examine next. In other words, they hope to leverage the goodwill associated with the Judeo-Christian Apology in order to profit, usually in the form of a comeback. And they want the whole process wrapped up in a Twitter cycle.

An apology can be an implement in a comeback, but it only marks the beginning of a longer journey.

The Transactional Apology

A Transactional Apology offers a display of repentance in exchange for something of tangible value. *I will apologize if you give me something that I want. In other words, in order to win a public acknowledgment of your forgiveness, which may or may not be sincere, I will pay you.*

A perfect example of a Transactional Apology was when Los Angeles Lakers basketball star Kobe Bryant apologized to a woman who had accused him of rape. On the eve of his criminal trial, his accuser decided not to testify. Bryant released a statement that read:

> Although I truly believe this encounter between us was consensual, I recognize now that she did not and does not view the incident the same way I did. After months of reviewing discovery, listening to her attorney and even her testimony in person, I now understand how she feels she did not consent to this encounter.

This "non-apology apology" almost surely came with a civil financial settlement with his accuser, which Bryant, with an NBA contract worth tens of millions of dollars, was in a position to pay. By taking this approach, he avoided trial, a potential conviction, and imprisonment. He also returned to basketball, where he enjoyed some of the highlights of his career.

The Transactional Apology is a great option if you've got it. Bryant's was preceded by a months-long series of media investigations of his accuser's alleged past drug use, emotional stability, sex life, and penchant for publicity. While no one knows how many of these discoveries were tied to the work of Bryant's defense team, it's safe to say that they weren't displeased by the dividends yielded.

Transactional Apologies are often seen in the civil and criminal settlements that individuals and institutions reach with their accusers whereby they admit little to no wrongdoing and pay fines in exchange for the resolution of litigation. Of course, these techniques are not truly apologies, but that is precisely the point: The accused participate in the theater of repentance in order to stop the pain.

The "Marital" Apology

Does it ever pay to apologize for something you did not do or that you do not believe that you did?

This is the question I pose to my business school students, and it always provokes lively debate. The visceral reaction is usually *No way!* Some students, recognizing that I am often hired to fight back on behalf of the scandal-plagued, believe I will instinctively share this hard-line view.

But I don't.

My job is to help clients survive their marketplace muggings, not to be an action hero. When the situation calls for a counteroffensive, and pushback has a chance of yielding success, I'll all for it. However, some cases are fraught with so much tension that there is no chance of a resolution until that tension is released.

Long-married people know this phenomenon well. Even though

it's not in the sanctioned marital relations handbook, there are times that you apologize even if you're not sure what you did wrong. Or even if you're convinced you were actually right in the first place. Tension is unpleasant, and sometimes attempts to communicate inflame rather than defuse. So you say you're sorry without reaching an intellectual understanding of what went wrong.

Enter the "Marital Apology," the one you issue just so you can move on.

Toyota wasn't guilty of manufacturing cars that took off like rockets of their own volition, but the vortex of allegations and devastating news coverage was so intense that if Toyota *didn't* apologize, the story would have become the company's hostility to consumer safety. Sometimes apologies have to be evaluated in the inverse: *not what the apology does, but what the absence of apology does.*

Getting principals to apologize in high-profile scandals has become a base-tagging exercise. If you tag the base in baseball, you get some credit for landing there, but not much else. If, however, you fail to tag it, you're out.

The chief venues of Toyota's apology were congressional hearings held in February 2010. Chief executive Akio Toyoda stated, "I am deeply sorry for any accidents that Toyota drivers have experienced. Especially, I would like to extend my condolences to the members of the Saylor family, for the accident in San Diego. I would like to send my prayers again, and I will do everything in my power to ensure that such a tragedy never happens again."

The call for these hearings acutely limited Toyota's options. Congressional hearings are reputational lynchings, not true legal forums or informational exchanges. They are opportunities for Congress to scold targets, not for those on the hot seat to articulate zinging comebacks, which only serve to make targets look like smart-asses in need of comeuppance.

None of this is to imply that Toyota did not feel sorry about the suffering of its customers. The company executives very likely did; however, the apology's wording stopped short of admitting having caused the problems, which would have been a staple of a Judeo-Christian Apology. It would have also triggered a liability nightmare. As we shall see, there is ample reason to believe that Toyota did not cause some of the more serious problems its vehicles were accused of.

Once a principal apologizes, the story's natural arc tends to swing back upward because at some point the punishment has achieved narrative exhaustion. The principal can then begin to rebuild.

The Limits of Apology

Race is the quicksand of scandals—notoriously difficult to survive. Think: *Seinfeld*'s Michael Richards's racially charged comedy club rant, which didn't help his receding career; Mel Gibson, whose blockbuster juggernaut has been on hold since his alcohol-fueled anti-Semitic tirade to a policeman in 2006; bail bondsman "Dog the Bounty Hunter," who lost his A&E TV show after using racial epithets in a telephone call with his son that had been recorded; radio shock jock Don Imus, who lost his CBS Radio show in 2007 after referring to the Rutgers women's basketball team as "nappy headed hos"—despite serial apologies.

Racism has no constituency to be leveraged, and nobody benefits from parsing it. There is no "yes, but"; no mitigating circumstances follow, especially if the words really escaped the principal's lips. Occasionally, if a well-known figure's core competency has a limited connection to public opinion, he or she may be able to keep his or her job, but little more. When Philadelphia Eagles wide receiver Riley Cooper was captured at a Kenny Chesney concert using a racial epithet in a confrontation with a security guard, he apologized profusely. This is unlikely, however, to win him product endorsements.

In a sex scandal, there are always parties lining up to defend principals with the "Americans are so prudish" chestnut, even though this hasn't really been true for years. A popular corporation may even find supporters in the form of employees or consumers who believe that a company like Toyota was railroaded by the government. But nobody wants to jump in front of the racial locomotive, especially corporate sponsors that don't want to be in the same galaxy as racial debates for reasons including morality, boycotts, and legal liability.

Paula Deen didn't stand a chance once the content of her deposition went public. There is a Cycle of Apology to which situations like Deen's tend to loosely adhere:

1. Allegation—Someone cries foul about an affront, often a powerful figure transgressing on a weaker one;
2. Proof—Evidence of the offense is produced, such as the release of Deen's deposition. (If there is no evidence, the

NBC Newswire/Getty Images

offense may be denied, and the crisis may end there depending upon what else turns up);

3. Apology—After evidence is produced, the principal apologizes, usually characterizing the offense. Deen tried this several times, including during her deposition, where she put her use of the epithet in the context of the times as well as the conditions under which she had used the term (she had been at gunpoint during a bank robbery);

4. Apology Flagged—In the Fiasco Vortex, the apology is almost always declared to have been fumbled or "too little too late." Deen's cancellation of a *Today* show mea culpa was criticized, as was an awkward video she released apologizing. A subsequent *Today* interview was better but also widely panned;

5. Head Rolling—Deen's contracts were terminated or not renewed by multiple sponsors and business partners. (In some cases like these, the principal voluntarily resigns.) At this writing, the Deen saga is stuck in this phase of the cycle;

6. Overkill/Backlash—Once the most intense part of the scandal passes, a sense of overkill finds its way into the discussion. If they're smart, principals keep a low profile, and a sentiment develops that they have been punished enough. Martha Stewart, Michael Vick, and Toyota benefited from this phenomenon;

7. The "Anti-Story"—Contrary facts about the controversy may emerge that put the original events in a broader context. Toyota's eventual vindication on the "sudden acceleration" allegations gave loyal consumers permission to revisit the brand, which they did in big numbers; and

8. Recovery—The principal reemerges, usually, but not always, with a smaller platform.

Through savvy crisis management, handlers can help adjust the margins of the Cycle of Apology by helping the principal time the news waves and exploit developments as they arise. Still, there is an organic component to the life cycle of controversy. To some degree, as with the stomach flu, the virus must be allowed to pass through the system before a recovery can take hold.

To fully appreciate the role that damage control clichés and apologies play in the midst of conflict, the chapter that follows offers insight into the multibillion-dollar industry that merchandizes these and other elixirs.

> **Takeaway:** Apologies mark the beginning of a recovery, not the conclusion. Before one embarks on a path of redemption, it pays to know which type of apology, if any, is right for the situation.

9

The "Spindustrial" Complex

"Advertising is in an odd position. Its extreme protagonists claim it
has extraordinary powers...and its severest critics believe them."

—ANDREW S. C. EHRENBERG

The Entertainment Culture Defines Reality

One of the strangest things that has occurred during my career
has been the deification, if not the eroticization, of the "spin doctor," or fixer. The spin doctor has become our American Merlin, an
occult action figure that can control the uncontrollable, the common attribute of our superheroes. There is the lethal *Ray Dono-
van* (Liev Schreiber) of the eponymous Showtime drama; the wily
and gorgeous Olivia Pope (Kerry Washington), who balances her
career with trysts with the president on ABC's *Scandal*; litigator
Harvey Spector (Gabriel Macht) of USA Network's *Suits*, who can
turn the tables back on his clients' critics with a cocked eyebrow;
The Good Wife's crisis manager Eli Gold (Alan Cumming), who can
easily spike a hatchet job with a tantrum; tobacco flack Nick Naylor
(Aaron Eckhart) of the book and film *Thank You for Smoking*; rab-
binical genius Conrad Brean (Robert De Niro) of the satire *Wag
the Dog*; *Pulp Fiction*'s fixer Winston Wolf (Harvey Keitel); Kathy

Bates's bimbo exterminator in *Primary Colors*; and George Clooney's lawyer/cleaner in *Michael Clayton*.

These works are great entertainment anchored in the same trope, always spoken with arch confidence: "I'll take care of it" or "It's handled," and sometimes punctuated by "I promise." The spin doctor in the modern conception is part criminal, part magician. But when you break down what some of these characters actually do for their clients, it's not that impressive: *Pulp Fiction*'s Wolf just hoses blood and brains off a couple of killers and drives the death car to a scrap dealer.

The challenge has become the influence that the entertainment culture wields over otherwise intelligent mortals embroiled in controversy. Fantasy now defines expectations. One of the most prescient one-liners from cinema is from *The Man Who Shot Liberty Valance*: "When the legend becomes fact, print the legend." It was uttered in the context of a reporter running with a version of events that was more attractive than the banal truth.

Just as gangsters began hugging and kissing each other *after* the release of *The Godfather* to emulate what they saw in the film (before that, they mostly shook hands), so have many in the spin world begun to cultivate the confidence of their fictional counterparts. I was asked to attend a hilarious meeting at the Georgetown office of someone I was told was a "fellow crisis manager" with whom there might be "synergies." I had never heard of him.

When I got there, a nice older woman escorted me into a windowless room with clocks displaying times in different cities. I found myself sitting across from a gimlet-eyed character with albino white hair who wore cuff links in the shape of a human skull. He had a blinking red telephone on his desk and had two henchmen standing behind him: One was wearing a black eye patch and the other had his wrist handcuffed to a briefcase.

I spent much of the meeting with my mouth covered because

I was afraid I was going to start laughing. There are few more suicidal moves than to laugh at a fraud, especially one posing as a James Bond villain; a fraud is more dangerous than the real deal because someone with actual power wouldn't have any interest in a charade like this, and a fraud's mission is to defend the lie that sustains him. Unfortunately, I hadn't worn my trusty shoes with the tear gas canisters in the heels or I might have made a quicker exit. Right, synergies.

So, this is what the business has become, I thought, as I said goodbye to Miss Moneypenny on my way out. I never saw them again.

The legend of spin doctors has actually become a standard expectation, and it is in no one's interest to throw cold water on it. The same news media that claim to abhor being spun love a good spin doctor story. The meme of a Svengali puppeteer pulling strings behind a curtain is a winning set piece that has the added luxury of being impossible to prove or disprove. As Michael Socolow wrote about Orson Welles's fabled 1938 radio airing of H. G. Wells's *The War of the Worlds*, "At the time, it cemented a growing suspicion that skillful artists—or incendiary demagogues—could use communications technology to capture the consciousness of the nation."

As charming people are easily charmed, the media world trades in legends of the "dark arts" because it is self-validating. It's nice to be in on the secret, provided that all the rubes never figure out there isn't one. An omniscient reporter wise enough to expose a spin doctor must be wise indeed.

If the public had any idea how often propaganda campaigns fail, it would be far less impressed. Oddly, one of the more trenchant summaries of real life as a fixer comes from the film *Michael Clayton* when, after a disappointed client demands the miracle he thought he was paying for, Clooney's Clayton tells him, "I'm not a miracle worker. I'm a janitor."

Barriers to Entry

A student recently asked me this question: What are the barriers to entry to the crisis management business?

I grappled for a professorial answer for a few seconds and finally surrendered: "Actually, none...except maybe a sport jacket and the ability to tick off platitudes as if you had obsessive-compulsive disorder—you know, 'trust,' apologies, and maybe a line or two about the Tylenol case...." I threw in a few more of the standard applause lines such as, "If you're in a hole, stop digging," and "our thoughts and prayers are with the [insert demographic you are empathizing with]."

"Like baboons sniffing each other in the Serengeti to make sure no interlopers have penetrated the troop," somebody said.

I wasn't quite so harsh. "Let's just say that with some outfits under siege, the objective seems to be to have a good meeting, which means nobody felt threatened by anybody recommending actions that could cost anybody their jobs...."

When I started in this field and told people my job, they would ask, "You can make a living doing that?" These days, it seems like everybody's in crisis management, especially the multinational advertising conglomerates.

And therein lies the problem.

The Big Scramble

Crisis management is a young discipline in the midst of a turbulent reinvention. All young fields are refined by experimentation, trial and error. The struggles of businesses, institutions, and prominent individuals in managing new challenges are not that different from those faced by medicine, science, and all endeavors that were once defined by beliefs and assumptions that turned out to be wrong.

Damage control is especially challenging to nail down because it is more art than science.

I am going to be hard on the advertising and communications consulting industry—I call it "Big PR"—which has annexed the crisis management discipline, not because it is diabolical, but because it is out of its depth in the crisis arena. The industry's flawed dogma anchors the popular understanding of how controversies are handled.

To fully appreciate how scandals are managed, it helps to understand the players in the priesthood of spin, what they are selling, and what they want their clients to believe they can accomplish. The two pillars that support Big PR are that controversy can be controlled using the services they sell and that the industry possesses a "special knowledge," inaccessible to outsiders, that can be deployed to exert that control. As John F. Kennedy said after the failure of the Bay of Pigs invasion, "You always assume that the military and intelligence people have some secret skill not available to ordinary mortals."

I admire the advertising discipline, once worked for a subsidiary of a large international advertising agency, and, in fact, partner with ad firms on campaigns with a crisis management component. However, there are fundamental problems and conflicts with the ad industry's annexation of damage control. This comes mostly in the form of the juggernaut of acquisitions by huge, publicly traded conglomerates.

The crux of the problem lies in how these consultancies make their money: the generation of content, including advertising, "earned" media placement, and social media outreach. Agencies are under pressure to sell these services to clients whether they need them or not. When I worked for an agency in the early 1980s, they made their money by charging a 15 percent commission on media buys. The margins are now a fraction of what they once were. The frenzy of mergers and acquisitions to create ever-expanding behemoths are engineered to demonstrate buying power to big advertisers who are increasingly tempted to bypass their agencies, make their own ads, and go straight to Google or Facebook.

Large PR firms, which are increasingly owned by these agencies, usually make their money by billing the time they work to create content and seek media coverage for their clients. Clients rightly demand to know what they are getting for all of this billed time. These factors, combined with the decline of old media and the rise of digital media, have led to a big scramble to convey relevance. This is especially true in the present climate, where big marketers are increasingly turning to the agencies that helped them *build* their brands for advice on how to prevent them from getting destroyed.

The pressure to serve clients in crisis in a disruptive marketplace has contributed to the overpeddling of the shiniest new object, social media. Social media is a form of content creation, which Big PR does very well. When it comes to marketing products, promoting events, or raising social awareness, it can have a lot of power. When it comes to defusing controversy, as we've seen, social media's utility is risky.

Big PR loves social media because it's something to sell. It's also immediate: You bang a few keys, look on the screen, and there it is. Proselytizing the mirage of social media as a crisis management solution is sufficiently vague that clients assume that if it's not working for them, they must be doing it wrong. Time to call in the experts.

Besieged principals are tempted by social media because it gives them the illusion of control, *of doing something*. The problem is, just because you can do it doesn't mean you should.

This Big Scramble has forced agencies that were once owned by client-focused entrepreneurs, who took a long-term view of relationships, to report numbers to profit-and-loss executives at holding companies on a quarterly basis, who must report these results to shareholders. Whether they were in advertising or PR, there was a greater love of the craft and commitment to the client twenty and thirty years ago, as opposed to the constant obsession with numbers that prevails now.

Overfitting

Big PR is not conspiring to mislead their clients into buying services they don't need. There are simply broad systemic incentives to recommend what they can sell versus what actually works—not unlike health-product hucksters who recommend treatments based upon whatever salve is in their pushcarts versus the ailment that their mark suffers from. This is "overfitting"—too many supposed solutions to solve specific problems (that they don't, in fact, solve). This means the kind of content creation programs that may work well in advertising and marketing but don't always apply to managing controversy.

As with any field where there is money to be made, crisis management has become commoditized. PR firms are now peddling cookie-cutter "reputation management" programs that claim to be able to prevent and defuse crises. It is the merchandizing of hope and it's not new to humankind, but it has come relatively recently to crisis management. This is why the industry perpetuates the myth of the perfectly managed Tylenol crisis and, now, the knee-jerk evangelizing of social media.

The people who create and leverage media content to become great marketers are not the same people who should be managing crises. The sales discipline rewards frequency, reflexivity, positivity, and enthusiasm more than it does nuance, discretion, deal making, patience, and political and legal tactics. As Nassim Nicholas Taleb writes in *The Black Swan*, "It's much easier to sell 'Look what I did for you' than 'Look what I avoided for you.'"

Big PR also rewards advice and advisors that are comforting and pose little risk to the client relationship. A counselor who trots out applause lines like "transparency" will fare better than one who demands an explanation of what that actually means in the context of the crisis at hand.

Who's the Client?

One of the biggest conflicts of interest posed by Big PR concerns the overreliance on media relations—systematic cooperation with the press even when it is not in the client's interest. For a PR pro who makes her living cultivating relationships with the press, does she feel a greater obligation to a crisis client that may be gone in a month or a journalist with whom she and her firm(s) may be doing business for decades?

It is in the best interest of the PR person, their firm, and its share-holders to maintain good relationships with the press. Clients hire PR firms because of their presumed relationships with reporters. Conflicts can be finessed by convincing clients that it is in *their* best interest to go on camera in the midst of controversy. This approach works for some principals but not others.

From a realpolitik standpoint, a big PR firm's clients are the media they need on an ongoing basis for those who pay them big fees. These relationships do benefit paying clients, but when the relationship between a client and investigative media become adversarial, the PR person may not be an authentic advocate for her client.

The conflict doesn't manifest itself through blatant betrayal. It's more subtle and even unconscious. I have been in many situations where PR firms counseled their clients to ramp up communication with hostile reporters to avoid offending them. This works sometimes. Other times, it provides fodder for media determined to take the client down.

The Opiate of Planning

Those facing scandal have a very human need to feel as if they can control their fates. The military strategist Helmuth von Moltke famously observed, "No plan of battle survives contact with the enemy." The same holds true for crisis plans. Bureaucracies abhor uncertainty and are susceptible to the notion that bad things happen because somebody failed to plan for them. Planning for certain eventualities is better than not planning, but modern controversies are hard to anticipate.

In the 1980s and 1990s, I wrote a lot of crisis management plans. Big, fat, long, detailed plans. I rarely do this anymore because most of the cases I get are unpredictable, and when a crisis hits, the plans prove worthless. They tend to overemphasize a neurotic contemplation of events, as if there will be an award for the sheer quantity of horrible things that can be conjured up.

Wrote General Norman Schwarzkopf, "Analysts write about war like it's choreographed ahead of time. Like the orchestra strikes up, and everyone goes out and plays a set piece. Sure, it's choreographed. But what happens is some son-of-a-bitch climbs out of the orchestra pit with a bayonet and starts chasing you around the stage. And the choreography goes right out the window."

Obsessive planning provides a false sense of security that comes with the fleshing out of busywork associated with each scenario and mistakes the length and detail of a plan with responsible stewardship. I haven't found that the creation of an exhaustive scenario document corresponds with effective crisis management. I do see that consulting firms profit by billing time creating useless what-if work that makes clients feel as if they are buying an insurance policy.

A plan is often a stand-in for taking meaningful action: Spending twenty thousand dollars on a document that outlines how to respond to a superficial catalyst is easier than examining the inherent risks or behaviors that may land you in trouble. It is also less disruptive than considering the complex and costly programs that will be needed to manage a chronic challenge.

A plan is only a plan if its true objective is to help disarm a bomb, not give those who commissioned it the illusion of having tackled a serious challenge.

For those encountering scandal, it is comforting to believe there is a playbook—and horrifying to think there isn't. The PR industry is adept at assuring clients that not only is there a playbook, but that they have it. When the business is pitched, the preferred technique is to assure the prospect that if things get nasty, their "positives" can be leveraged. This is appealing because it doesn't require the client to alter behavior, just be more assertive about promoting their flattering attributes (*"The real problem here is that you don't realize how awesome you are…"*). A program like this is often supplemented by promoting a pleasantly fuzzy virtue like "trust," which no one opposes, but whose value to the scandal management is equally opaque.

Meta-Spin

The entertainers Madonna and Lady Gaga have made part of their personal narratives their shape-shifting proclivities, but everyone is fine with this because they are entertainers and we are all players in the hoax. Nobody gets hurt. It is in the celebrity media's interest to promote these entertainers' transformational brilliance because it serves as yet another hook to cover them. This occurs in the same spirit that audiences know that magicians aren't really sawing women in half, but the spectacle of watching the process unfold is still riveting.

When a politician or corporation starts spinning, however, the public is on guard because we are potential victims. Not everybody is allowed to play us, but while we are being unsuccessfully played, we long to believe there are those with the power to do it. The subversive power to spin the public is the news hook that facilitates the self-generation of additional stories about mind control.

There are now entire media beats devoted to covering spin. Bill O'Reilly declares his prime-time cable show the "no spin zone." Cable television shows dissect the PR tactics of politicians, governments, celebrities, and businesses on an hourly basis. One of the stranger concepts in the evolution of spin is the "spin room," which emerges after presidential debates and other campaign milestones. Spin rooms consist of campaign loyalists who debrief the press after a big event, inevitably declaring that their candidate won. No reporter who attends these farces believes he is going to learn anything worthwhile, but they attend to snag a quote, capture a stressed-out flack saying something inflammatory, or report on the spin phenomenon itself (in other words, "Here is how the body snatchers are trying to spin you today...").

In the coverage of Wall Street crises, corporate spin gurus leverage the media to boost their own credentials for TV show bookers so that they can be invited back for further bookings. It is typical for the TV host to ask the pundit to "grade" the principal's handling of the crisis. A grade of C– or lower assures an invitation to come back and slam the next poor target. This wisdom rarely serves as legitimate analysis as much as it does marketing. Consultants with a blue-chip client base rarely disclose how they really helped solve a client's problem because the truth is either confidential, not interesting, or could come back to bite them.

Controversies are not isolated matters of actions and reactions. In the Fiasco Vortex, the reaction becomes part of the action; the self-amplifying meta-crisis cannot be separated from the crisis because the media analysis feeds it. Punditry creates a media greenhouse effect that intensifies the scandal.

The phenomenon of "second screen" watching has become a critical factor in the amplification of controversy. The term "second screen" originally referred to television viewers watching both a program and simultaneously following Internet reviews, recaps, and chat rooms for this program. This now applies to consumers of controversy who are following both factual developments and what supposed experts are saying about the *handling* of the controversy. The farce surrounding the controversy becomes bigger than the actual

How did this happen?
Who's to blame?

How 2 inches of snow froze city

Atlanta's mayor and Georgia's governor blame everyone trying to get home at the same time for the storm traffic nightmare. But there's more to it than that. FULL STORY

• Governor changes his tune
• Traffic eases — helping out —
• Mayor responds to criticism —
• Opinion where hell freezes over

CNN screen capture

controversy, which is precisely what happened after the January 2014 snowstorm that snarled Atlanta: So begins the hunt for "suspects."

The media thrive on instantaneous representations of causation. When the stock market rises or falls, coverage characterizes it as having "moved *on*" a jobs report or an overseas event. The scramble for causation assumes that there is a singular cause and that the expert who has been summoned has special insight into that cause. We assume this to be the case by virtue of their availability, as opposed to their qualifications. The cries to lynch the principal are simply the Fiasco Vortex's equivalent of the primitive legend of throwing a virgin in the volcano to appease an angry god.

The debate that ensues during a controversy lurches toward hyperbole. When Toyota has a recall, the question posed is, "Can Toyota survive?" (Of course it can.) In a matter of weeks, Apple swings from being celebrated as the newly crowned most valuable company in the world to being the subject of debates about its impending oblivion. These swings, encouraged by the media and pundits, infect the controversy on multiple levels—morale, investor confidence, political, defection of customers and allies. In the Fiasco Vortex, there is no "in between," only extremes of genius and incompetence, meteoric rises and crashes to earth.

When JetBlue canceled 1,100 flights during a blizzard in 2007, I did a television interview where I was asked by the on-air talent why I thought JetBlue had such a mess on its hands. I answered, "One reason is because you keep inviting guests on and asking them why JetBlue has such a mess on its hands." The company's CEO, David Neeleman, the point man in the controversy, was unseated after the mess.

I decided shortly after this experience to sharply curtail my media appearances discussing scandals because I did not want to fight in the battle to reach the lowest common denominator. This state is best achieved by covering spectacles, real and manufactured, supported by on-air guests who will fuel the circus by excoriating the players.

It is the triumph of shock over expertise. I don't want to accelerate somebody else's crisis by identifying human piñatas. You can't be in my business for as long as I have and not develop a deep empathy for what people under attack go through. In the increasingly rare cases where I believe I can provide a constructive media analysis, I participate.

Industry in a Bubble

I have often debated this question with colleagues: Are spin doctors lying about their powers or do they truly believe in them? The catechism of spin is largely a function of muscle memory, belief perseverance, and being part of a priesthood that reinforces a certain creed. Like many professions, the PR industry is insular and self-quoting. Firms buy advertising space in trade publications to reinforce their expertise, and they are occasionally given awards or guest columns by these publications.

PR industry leaders cite the same case studies that reinforce the correlation between PR tactics and the successful resolution of crises. The Praetorian Guards at some of these trade publications are hostile to case studies that question the dominant dogma and those who don't identify their clients or share case studies.

I suspect that the PR discipline is chronically afraid of its own obsolescence. For the past thirty years, conferences and newsletters have been replete with whining about the lack of respect PR receives from top management. Many communicators either truly believe in their powers or are afraid not to. This anxiety is especially intense against the backdrop of a disruptive landscape. Contrary to the popular conception of PR people as evil geniuses, most communicators earnestly link their skills with notions about the benevolence of their work.

If the spin industry is such a racket, how can I justify being in it for more than three decades? There is an old saw about how half of advertising is wasted, but nobody knows which half. The point is that you still have to advertise. This applies to damage control.

I figure that three-quarters of crisis management ends up being useless, one-quarter has some value, and, of that quarter, about 5 percent could be pivotal. Client expectations of crisis managers are rising, but what can actually be done during scandals is falling because of the Fiasco Vortex.

DEZENHALL CONTROVERSY METRICS:
EXPECTATIONS MUST INTERSECT WITH WHAT IS ACHIEVABLE

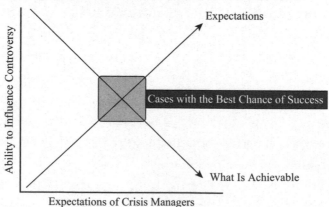

The challenge is that at the beginning of an engagement, it is hard to know which elements will be the ones that contribute to a principal's redemption, so you must throw a lot at the case before you know what's working.

The reason that I am selective about the projects I take on is that I can only be effective in a limited percentage of them. I have learned to profile potential clients with an eye toward those I can help and those I cannot. The best clients are large corporations or institutions that have endured controversy before and have: a strong, small, and improvisational leadership team directly engaged in the crisis-at-hand; a realistic appreciation of their liabilities and how these weaknesses will be perceived; a strong counternarrative (or resolution) to the current allegations; and budgets unfettered by demands for immediate outcomes.

The "red flags" that portend failure include: sweeping denials of allegations in the face of contrary evidence; promises of exculpatory information that never comes; obsessing over collateral inaccuracies that fail to dispute the core charges; limited access to decision makers; management-by-committee and warring consultants (and a history of hopping from advisor to advisor); a belief that the cure lies in retaining the right player who can put the "fix" in; unrealistic expectations; and limited resources.

One of the chief commodities of Big PR is "reputation," as if it can be manufactured and sold like cereal. But can it be? And, if so, what exactly does a good reputation *mean* in a crisis management exercise? We will address this in the following chapter.

> **Takeaway:** In crisis management, the experts may not be experts at all, and may, in fact, be obstacles to a successful resolution. It's important to understand the true loyalties and capabilities of the expanding universe of self-styled fixers.

10

The Myth of Reputation Management (Whatever That Means)

"This is like dogs chasing a rabbit. When the rabbit wins, he doesn't get to kill the dogs and eat them. He doesn't get to be a dog. He just gets to keep being a rabbit."

—*VANISHING ACT*, THOMAS PERRY

Next to social media mania, "reputation management" is the latest engrossment in corporate communications. One of its tactical manifestations is achieving a high ranking on magazine lists of most admired companies or the best places to work. These rankings are thought to positively affect personnel recruiting, employee and shareholder morale, and even consumer affection for a company. And they may to some degree, in part because these lists have become self-fulfilling prophecies. The perception that lists matter has had the effect of making them matter.

To make such lists, companies often campaign expending significant resources to demonstrate that they excel in the various ranking criteria such as innovation, employee retention, social responsibility, and people management. This tends to reward the capacity to merchandize flashy attributes much in the same way that Ivy League college applicants are more likely to market themselves as future Nobel Peace Prize contenders versus the investment bankers they are more likely to become.

Other reputation management techniques are designed to protect a business or individual's "downside" and help them get back to business—or their lives. Think of the three Duke University lacrosse players who were falsely accused of rape in 2006. They were cleared of the charges after an intense legal and PR counteroffensive, but they will forever be associated with a crime that didn't happen.* The allegations will be held against them by the kind of detractors many of us encounter in one form or another during our lives: future spouses, in-laws, and employers will harbor twinges of doubt, and someday their children will learn on the Internet of the allegations that were once leveled against them. But they are free men, no small achievement.

When Reputation Is a Fetish Not a Strategy

In a book I wrote with my longtime business partner John Weber, *Damage Control*, we were critical of BP's "Beyond Petroleum" advertising campaign several years *before* the 2010 oil spill on the grounds that the company was posing as an alternative energy company when it really wasn't. Our belief was that this massive goodwill campaign to draw attention to its solar and wind power programs had backfire potential in the event of an adverse incident. Our actual words: "Will the public and [BP's] most vocal critics feel betrayed if, years from now, BP hasn't really gotten beyond petroleum after all? Has BP been too clever for its own good? Time will tell."

---

* This counteroffensive was expensive. Defendants of lesser family means may never have been vindicated at all.

Time told. After the oil spill, the company was slammed for expending so many resources on public relations that glorified comparatively marginal efforts to grow its solar and wind businesses. Journalists were enraged, many feeling that the company had conducted the Beyond Petroleum campaign to paper over its environmental shortcomings. However unfair, this is an example of what can happen when a company develops a fetish for reputation control that exceeds what it has the capacity to deliver in the way of tangible progress.

Exxon (now ExxonMobil) took a very different approach to reputation management after being attacked for its handling of the 1989 *Exxon Valdez* oil spill. In the decades since *Valdez*, ExxonMobil has anchored its damage control efforts in revamping its approach to safety rather than puffery. Its initiatives aren't sexy, but they seem to be working: For an oil company, the best reputation management is the *absence* of adverse incidents, and ExxonMobil hasn't had a major once since *Valdez*. Its Operations Integrity Management System program contains eleven elements that address prevention, security, test drills, management accountability, and proprietary technology that seeks to predict the pressure and flow of wells. Two new double-hulled supertankers are entering service presently.

In an age of insipid self-congratulation, the contrast between ExxonMobil and BP begs the question: Is it more "sustainable" to quietly bolster your environmental safety practices or tout alternative energy fantasies that aren't really occurring in a meaningful way?

Banking giant Goldman Sachs found itself in the hot seat after the 2008 financial meltdown over the company's role in the packaging of subprime mortgages. Pundits criticized the company for not having done more over its century and a half in business to endear itself to the public. Never mind that Goldman and financial behemoths like it do little to no business directly with the public and have no emotionally resonant narrative in which to endear themselves to mass audiences. We've all heard the argument that banks play an important role in generating prosperity and jobs, and this is true. The problem is that this rational argument is overwhelmed by the deeply emotional bias against any enterprise that earns unfathomable amounts of money in a complicated (read: diabolical) way.

After the financial meltdown, Goldman communicated about how it contributes to businesses in small communities, but it shrewdly recognized that it stood a better chance of being targeted a little bit less than being loved a whole lot more. After months of speculation that it would be criminally indicted or be forced to forfeit tens of billions of dollars because of its subprime mortgage dealings, Goldman agreed to a $550 million settlement with the Securities and Exchange Commission. This civil settlement did not require the company to plead guilty to any crimes, but Goldman did express regret for not disclosing certain aspects of marketing a particular subprime product.

The deal was criticized from many quarters, including some that argued that the settlement would not improve Goldman's reputation. Perhaps, but knocking this unpleasant chapter out of the headlines helped the bank get back to business and mitigate scrutiny from a number of parties, mainly the government, that were in a position to hurt it.

Goldman wisely realized that sometimes the objective of crisis management is not to get audiences to like you, but to get them to stop attacking you—or move on to another target.

The Arc of Michael Vick

Quarterback Michael Vick, then of the Atlanta Falcons, earned the wrath of the republic when he was prosecuted for running an illegal dogfighting ring. This operation included the drowning and electrocution of dogs, not to mention the horrible injuries and death caused by the fighting itself. Vick's crisis management skills were savaged in the press. Vick apologized, served as a spokesperson for the Humane Society's anti-dogfighting campaign in the inner cities, and went to prison for nineteen months, going bankrupt in the process.

Upon Vick's release, the Philadelphia Eagles signed him, and he had a very successful first season. Much was made of Vick's brilliant image makeover. As with Martha Stewart, Vick didn't actually *have* an image makeover. His comeback was one part by-product of the judicial system that sent him to jail, one part by-product of his athletic skills. Sure, he apologized. What else was he going to do, announce that nothing beats the thrill of electrocuting defenseless puppies? Furthermore, reading the signals coming out of the National Football League, if Vick wanted to return to football, a decision that was in the league's hands, it would be in his best interest to volunteer for the Humane Society, which he did.

Did Vick's reputation really improve? According to a recent *Forbes* survey, he was the most disliked player in the NFL. Very little that he did actually changed the minds of the public. However, being universally loved wasn't Vick's best *achievable* outcome: Being able to play in the NFL was. The key audiences for his outreach were the courts, which had the power over his liberty, and the NFL, which determined his eligibility to play.

Vick's comeback contained elements that were in and out of his control. He was *forced* to go to jail. His animal welfare efforts may have been sincere, but they had a compulsory element. It wasn't as if his Humane Society work caused people to conclude that Vick was a true animal rights activist. As John F. Kennedy responded to a question about how he became a war hero: "It was involuntary. They sank my boat."

Perhaps the only factor in Vick's recovery that can truly be ascribed to brilliance was his capacity as an athlete. As with most comebacks, Vick's had more to do with his core skill set than the wizardry of those off the gridiron. Accordingly, Lance Armstrong can do apologia road shows for the rest of his life, but he won't make a dent in his reputation as an athlete unless he wins the Tour de France a few more times without steroids. The same concept holds true for slugger Barry Bonds, who never came back from his steroid scandal.

Moonwalking to a Better Image?

I was a member of a legal team that worked on Michael Jackson's defense when the entertainer was accused of child molestation in 2003.* There was a meeting early in the process, before the allegations went public, about how a crisis manager might assist in the effort.

This was an important discussion because we must deal with the client we are given as opposed to who we want him to be. This includes navigating personalities and variables that are difficult to control. From the time he was a little boy, Michael Jackson knew that the presence of a camera signaled it was time to perform. This is why he agreed to the interview with British journalist Martin Bashir where he unhelpfully defended having sleepovers with children. He knew which of his handlers would let him perform in certain environments and which ones would not, so he was highly selective about whom he advised of his intentions. Those who said "yes" tended to enjoy longer employment.

At his arraignment, the entertainer spontaneously hopped up onto an SUV and posed for his fans, including a dance move or two,

---

* My role in this case was made public—not by me—during the trial. I have never commented on it publicly, nor will I disclose anything here that violates any confidences or privileged discussions.

something that a few pundits implied was part of a clever PR campaign. Wrong: The SUV incident was the impulse of an entertainer whose muscle memory dictated that he should perform when there were cameras on him.

This was an example of how doing what one does best may be great on some stages but destructive on others. There isn't much that can be done to restrain the mega-famous, rich, and powerful from being faithful to their natures.

In this early discussion about the role of crisis management, a publicist expressed concern that many people thought of Jackson as being weird, and how it would be hard to get his career back on track if this image persisted.

"He *is* weird," I said. "Either that or his perceived weirdness was carefully cultivated and is now baked into the casserole of his identity. I can't undo that."

The publicist said, "Then what are we bothering with you for?"

Jackson's counsel at that time, Mark Geragos, understood where I was going with this. A seasoned defense attorney, Geragos operated in an environment of stark reality and guided Jackson through a precarious period of his ordeal.

Again, I asked what else those assembled thought a crisis manager could *actually* do. Someone else lamented, "Fewer and fewer people these days even remember *Thriller* [Jackson's bestselling album, released in late 1982] and his heyday."

"I can't bring back the early 1980s," I said.

Frustrated, another team member asked me what *I* thought crisis management could accomplish. I thought the objective was to support Jackson's bid for acquittal. If he went to jail, he couldn't sing and dance, and if he couldn't sing and dance, he couldn't pay down his significant debts.

Acquittal results from the doctrine of "reasonable doubt."

Jackson had attracted all kinds of vultures and extortionists, who contributed to both his indictment and his acquittal. He was acquitted because the jury had reasonable doubts that he had committed crimes. That his alleged victim had denied that Michael had molested him hurt the prosecutor's case. His accuser's family's history, which included his mother having charged that a JCPenney security guard molested her son, for which she secured a $150,000 payday, further sidelined the prosecution. The mother was eventually convicted of fraud for refusing to report his settlement income while collecting welfare.

Jackson's legal team emphasized in court, and in the limited media forums where it was able to participate, that there were good reasons to harbor reasonable doubts about the prosecution's version of events. It is impossible to determine the extent to which the focus on these themes outside of court contributed to the decisions the judge and jury made inside the courtroom. Nevertheless, in an age where legal and public opinion machinery intermingle, no savvy defense team will permit the media debate to be dominated solely by the prosecution, which has a big advantage in the realm of public opinion. Moreover, when the client is a public figure, he must challenge the falsehoods introduced during the course of litigation if he intends to return to a public career.

Despite Jackson's acquittal, his supporters and revolving door of advisors didn't radically improve his reputation, but that had never been the objective. The objective had been to support Jackson's case for acquittal because failing to do so would have left an enormous obstacle in the path of his rehabilitation.

Sadly, Jackson's reprise never happened during his lifetime, but after his acquittal, he won the confidence of major financial backers for a comeback tour. He had been rehearsing for this tour when he died of a drug overdose.

The "Trust Bank"

In the 1980s, I heard an impressive speaker use the term "trust bank." He was referring to a company's goodwill, something he said the company could "borrow against" in times of crisis. I thought it was brilliant and incorporated it into my thinking. It seemed so intuitive: The more people like you, the more you can ask them to forgive your missteps.

In time, I found that the trust bank theory did not hold up under fire. Having a "good reputation" did not shield targets from being sucked into a Fiasco Vortex. I like to compare sentiments like trust to "intermittent energy sources" such as solar, wind, and tidal power, elements that have to actually be present in order to be harnessed. One cannot simply summon trust any more than sunlight can be summoned at night to shine down on solar panels.

In fact, in some cases, the squeakier-clean the principals' reputation—think Johnson & Johnson, Susan G. Komen for the Cure, and Tiger Woods—the *harder* they may fall in the wake of a revelation that contradicts their reputation. As we remember from grade school, there is a deep impulse to step on the feet of the kid wearing shiny new shoes. Similarly, there is a powerful desire to see big shots take a pratfall—and few people care about yesterday's triumphs.

Goodwill and reputation are too conceptually abstract to defuse intense controversies, which tend to be based upon something tangible. "Corporate social responsibility" (CSR), voluntary efforts on the part of businesses to self-regulate by promoting programs such as philanthropy, environmental sustainability, and humanitarian aid, is worthwhile but not an inoculation against controversy. Engage in CSR programs because you believe in them and want to establish good works as being part of your or your company's identity, but I see no evidence that CSR is a mitigating factor when their sponsors become subjects of controversy.

If corporate goodwill is abstract and ethereal, brand loyalty is a different thing altogether. Consumer affection for Apple, Toyota, and Tesla *products* have helped their respective resiliencies in times of difficulty. Product loyalty is intimate and personal; consumers perceive a direct benefit whereas corporate goodwill is a passive, fuzzy sentiment.

Most people intuitively understand individual and organizational contradictions: A person can be an embezzler and still love his children, and a company can support charities and still make unsafe products. If you like your auto brand, however, you, well, like your car and will look for permission to keep driving it.

Another problem with the trust bank concept is the difference between being liked and being trusted. Very few people trusted Bill Clinton, but lots of people liked him enough to want him to remain president.

The Circus Fights Back on the Substance

Litigation or "lawfare"—fighting extralegal battles using the courts—is a favorite device of issue-warriors provided that the case doesn't have to endure the rigor of legal proceedings. Lawfare is a harassment device engineered to make the principal spend money and suffer sufficient embarrassment to change their policies. It is also a fund-raising and publicity tool. Issue-warriors rest assured that media coverage will trumpet the filing of most lawsuits against the principal and ignore their losses or dismissals.

This dynamic changes, however, when the rare target is willing to expend significant time, energy, and money fighting detractors peddling dubious allegations.

An extraordinary case of a company defending its reputation through a relentless pursuit of justice is that of Ringling Bros. and Barnum & Bailey Circus, which fought the false allegations of animal abuse brought by a handful of animal rights groups—and won.

Animal rights groups have been fighting against the use of animals in entertainment and agriculture for decades, using tactics such as infiltrating animal care facilities, filing frivolous lawsuits, making criminal allegations, and provoking large animals in order to capture animal handlers restraining them. Then, when the handlers restrain the animal, the activists misrepresent the action as being abusive. The very act of forcing a circus to answer a question about the abuse of an animal is a tactical win for activists because the poison has been introduced into the conversational bloodstream.

In 2000, a handful of animal rights groups banded together with a former Ringling Bros. employee to sue the circus under the Endangered Species Act, alleging that elephants were being abused. The groups included the American Society for the Prevention of Cruelty to Animals (ASPCA) and the Fund for Animals, among others. Knowing that Ringling Bros. was in the animal business, what better way to injure them than to allege animal cruelty to spectators who go to the circus to see exotic animals?

After nearly a decade of litigation, a federal court decided that the former circus employee had been on the payroll of the plaintiffs to the tune of at least $190,000 and was not credible, and it threw out the case.

Feld Entertainment, which owns Ringling Bros., decided to sue the animal rights groups for racketeering, conspiracy, and lawsuit abuse-related counts. In January 2013, the ASPCA settled with Feld for $9.3 million—*meaning the ASPCA had to pay that money to Feld/ Ringling Bros.* The company spent more than $20 million on the litigation. Litigation with the other animal rights groups is pending.

The media covered the landmark settlement extensively.

The coverage was vastly favorable to Ringling Bros., an unusual development because the media tend to cover animal rights activism with great sympathy. This case was different for a few reasons. Many reporters felt betrayed by the animal rights groups that had brought the initial lawsuit. The suit had originally been covered at face value, the allegations of animal mistreatment having been accepted as legitimate. When the media learned that the leading witness had been a paid plaintiff, they felt conned.

The media had also been intrigued that Ringling Bros. sued the animal rights groups that had made the original allegations in court. Suing a special-interest group would be a nonstarter in most businesses. The expense and, more important, the bad publicity would be enough to shut down any contemplation of litigation. The inverted nature of this turn of events demonstrates that a corporate victim can take meaningful action to defend itself.

The results of this case were unique both because of their merits and the nature of Feld Entertainment. Feld is a privately held, family-run business, now with its third generation working at the company. Impresario Irvin Feld brought the Ringling Bros. circus from near obscurity in the late 1960s. His son, Kenneth, built the firm into the largest live entertainment company in the world, encompassing Disney on Ice, Siegfried and Roy, monster trucks, and Broadway shows. Today, Kenneth Feld's daughters play leadership roles in the business.

But there was more to this case than sentimentality. Animal acts play a big role in the circus's history and culture, especially Asian elephants. There are very few venues where large audiences can experience rare elephants in person. Furthermore, elephants in the much-romanticized "wild" are routinely slaughtered by poachers. If Ringling intended to keep animals in its live acts, it could not allow the handlers who have devoted their careers to animal welfare to be assailed with impunity. Said Kenneth Feld upon the settlement,

"Animal activists have been attacking our family, our company, and our employees for decades because they oppose animals in circuses. This settlement is a vindication not just for the company but also for the dedicated men and women who spend their lives working and caring for all the animals with Ringling Bros."

The personal commitment of the Feld family to their enterprise is directly related to their strongly held belief that the Ringling Bros. circus is an American icon worthy of being preserved and defended. This rarely occurs in public companies, where inaction is the rule because no one perceives that it is in their interest to venture into the quagmire of controversy. It's a whole different story when a beloved grandfather rescued an American institution from oblivion; a son grew it from a national endearment into the global leader in its field; a third generation assumes greater responsibility in its direction; and a nascent fourth generation will now be steeped in its traditions.

Among the factors that determine one's reputation are the instinctive biases that precede scandal catalysts. In other words, we may have made up our minds long before we hear anything about an allegedly naughty company or public figure. We will look through this mysterious and hardwired prism next.

Takeaway: "Reputation" is a vital but abstract concept. Reputations are defended in the context of specific events, achievements, and brand loyalties—and must be faithful to what people know to be true about all three. Sometimes the best way to defend a reputation is to discreetly mitigate conflict or, when that isn't possible, to demonstrate that damaging allegations are false rather than trying to promote vague corporate, product, or personal virtues.

THE PHYSICS OF CONTROVERSY

11

Controversy Shortcuts and Cascades

Sam: It must be getting near tea-time, leastways in decent places where there *is* still tea-time.

Gollum: We're not *in* decent places.

J. R. R. TOLKIEN, *THE LORD OF THE RINGS*

Controversies have become self-feeding phenomena with their own gravities and ecosystems, operating in their own capricious environments. They are not inert objects in sterile laboratories with known reactions to long-researched chemicals. As chemistry teacher Walter "Heisenberg" White proved in AMC's hit series *Breaking Bad*, what he could brilliantly create in a methamphetamine lab did not translate into sustaining an empire where he had to interact with living creatures with brains, hearts, and whims in highly charged environments. Many scandal principals are stricken with a sense of failure when their own embroilment concludes badly. The fallacy here is that the only explanation for a disappointing outcome is their poor decision making (or bad consultants).

In most crises, there are things that could have been done better, and reflection is constructive. Most high-stakes situations include experimental actions—some effective, some not—and we do our best to make more good decisions than bad ones. <u>Still, many disaster variables remain in the hands of external forces.</u>

The word "disaster" derives from the Latin "dis," which means "away from," and "astro," which refers to the stars. In other words, a "disaster" means being far away from good luck. The ancients, it seems, actually understood better than we do the role that uncontrollable factors play in scandals. Given how many Americans tie individuality to destiny, we tend to discount the concept of luck. Many just don't believe that luck is a factor at all, especially the very successful, who are fond of trading in the self-congratulation, "You make your own luck." Friedrich Nietzsche countered with, "No victor believes in chance." Perhaps the more you hustle, the more you can capitalize on lucky breaks, but in every case of crisis resolution or avoidance, I have found luck to be a key variable.

The less control we have in the Fiasco Vortex, the more we gravitate to counterfactual non-options, the conceit being that there was an antidote to the crisis, but the principal failed to implement it. I'll repeat: Why would the richest, smartest, and most powerful people in the world consistently fail to resolve their crises if the rules of thumb were so easily applied?

We Think in Stories

Psychologists refer to convenient rules of thumb as "heuristics." In scandals, "availability heuristics" are snap judgments or mental shortcuts that spring easily to mind. They are *available* because they don't require the mind to process complex or banal data. A shortcut just "feels right," even if it's wrong.

Storytelling from time immemorial is filled with mental shortcuts. In his history of storytelling, *The Seven Basic Plots*, Christopher Booker highlights the main themes that inevitably turn up in folk tales, books, poems, plays, and filmed entertainment. Those "basic

Where's Love? Friendship?

plots" include: 1) Overcoming the Monster, 2) Rags to Riches, 3) The Quest, 4) Voyage and Return, 5) Comedy, 6) Tragedy, and 7) Rebirth.

The plot that most applies to scandal is "Overcoming the Monster." This plot pits a hero with ordinary qualities against an all-powerful, gratuitously wicked villain. Think *Beowulf, Star Wars*, James Bond, *Jaws*, and many Disney films. The audience needs the hero to smite the villainous monster because it is a threat to the rest of us. We also want the hero to win for reasons beyond self-preservation: The hero resembles us, and it's comforting to see someone with everyday qualities capable of great feats to seize control over his fate.

Hollywood exploits mental shortcuts by casting overweight, middle-aged men with deep southern accents as racist cops, beautiful blond women as criminal seductresses, and handsome men, wholesome women, and spunky kids as heroes. Even if a writer doesn't appear to be using shortcuts and casts a cute child as the monster, it's only because the real monster has possessed the child (*The Exorcist*).

Large organizations and powerful individuals, as opposed to mythical beasts such as *The Odyssey*'s Cyclops, are predestined to serve as villains in the present-day imagination. Think of these films and television shows (some based on books) where the corporation is the monster, to name a few: *Erin Brockovich, The Rainmaker, A Civil Action, Silkwood, Michael Clayton, The Fugitive, The China Syndrome, The Matrix, The Net, Damages, Prison Break, Blade Runner, Robocop, Eternal Sunshine of the Spotless Mind, Resident Evil, The Constant Gardner, Despicable Me, Ferngully, The Company Men, Avatar, Up in the Air, Inception, The Insider, The Devil's Advocate, Tomorrow Never Dies, The Manchurian Candidate* (remake), and even *Jurassic Park* and *Alien*, where mutant creatures stand in for the corporate greed of resort developers and a space conglomerate. There may also be an evolutionary basis for being afraid of big powerful creatures or institutions, which is why these themes resonate.

When corporations are shortcut villains, it doesn't take much to get the Fiasco Vortex spinning, especially in the wake of notorious examples from real life.

In order to overcome the monster, we need to first see the villain in action so we understand its capacity for mayhem. Our hero must then, after her imperilment is established, identify the monster's weakness and exploit it. The triumph cannot be easy, because if it is, the monster will lose its menace, and the victory won't be cherished with the intensity the audience demands. This is why Anthony Hopkins is scariest as Dr. Hannibal "the Cannibal" Lecter when he is caged behind thick glass or restrained with a mask that renders his jaws immobile. *What would this beast be capable of unfettered?*

Scandal Shortcut Classics

In real cultural narratives, proof of a monster's lethality need not be established by a demonstration of facts. To qualify as a shortcut, it needs only to confirm an existing worldview. The Kennedy assassination is a powerful cultural shortcut because it is much easier to fathom that a shadowy cabal of bad guys penetrated the defenses of the most powerful nation on earth than it is to believe that one loser with good aim pulled the trigger. That no one has been able to locate the multiple conspirators who supposedly accomplished this is de facto proof of their cleverness.

The Paula Deen affair is a shortcut masterpiece. In addition to her 2013 racial epithet uproar, the year before she had also found herself in an unwanted controversy when she announced, in 2012, that she had type 2 diabetes. This had been diagnosed a few years prior. Diabetes is often linked to the fatty and sugary diets Deen promotes. If the diabetes debacle didn't trigger outrage from cultural elites against this old-fashioned southern woman, her racially charged language was sure to.

The archetype Deen represented made it more plausible that she was guilty of the claims of discrimination that were made in the lawsuit. Despite the age of Deen's remarks—thirty years—something that one would think might render them irrelevant, they were deemed newsworthy in part because of mental shortcuts. The story just *seemed* right all the way around.

Deen's contract with the Food Network was not renewed, and she lost (or had suspended) endorsement deals with Smithfield Foods, Wal-Mart, QVC, Target, and Sears, in addition to her contract for multiple books.

In August 2013, a judge dismissed the racial discrimination component of the suit. The rest of the case was settled out of court later that month for an undisclosed amount. Both the dismissal and the settlement received a fraction of the media coverage that the contents of the deposition did. Deen is smartly keeping a low profile for now, and if she returns to prominence, it will likely be on a much smaller platform than she once enjoyed.

Another lifestyle doyenne, London-based Nigella Lawson, found herself in the headlines a few months after Deen, albeit for very different reasons. The catalysts of an ugly divorce and testimony in a former employee's fraud trial brought out two disturbing story lines. One involved allegations of spousal abuse, which was accompanied by a photo of her mogul husband with his hand around Lawson's neck. The other was a report of cocaine use, which Lawson admitted.

Shortcuts didn't affect Lawson's career as adversely as Deen's. If racism dovetailed perfectly with preexisting suspicions about Deen, neither Lawson's divorce nor her admission of cocaine use was a violation that conflicted with the chef's voluptuous style. Mental shortcuts took us to a place where Lawson's travails may have even been *expected* of a modern celebrity with her brand. That she appeared to be a victim of domestic abuse—as opposed to a generator of pain—also worked to her advantage.

Duck Dynasty patriarch Phil Robertson faced similar shortcuts to Deen when his disapproving remarks about homosexuality were published in a magazine interview at the height of his television show's popularity. A long-bearded, southern, devout Christian duck hunter opining on this subject—concurrent with historic gay rights legal and policy advancements—stomped on cultural live wires. The A&E TV network, which airs *Duck Dynasty*, suspended Robertson, but after many consumers expressed anger over his punishment, believing he had simply stated his religious views, supporters such as restaurant chain Cracker Barrel decided to keep selling *Duck Dynasty* merchandise. A&E reinstated Robertson.

New Jersey governor Chris Christie had been hailed as the Republican Party's savior and possible 2016 presidential nominee. Weeks after the pinnacle of his coronation in his reelection, news broke that his administration "gleefully engineered George Washington Bridge lane closures to punish the Democratic mayor of Fort Lee for failing to endorse their boss' [Christie] reelection," reported the *New York Daily News*. Amid the gridlock, in one instance emergency crews were unable to respond to calls about a gravely ill ninety-one-year-old woman, who later died. This story blessed the shortcut that Christie was 1) an archetypal New Jersey bully, 2) vindictive and self-obsessed, as opposed to being a "man of the people", 3) thin-skinned and adept at throwing punches but not absorbing them, and therefore not ready for the national stage, and 4) just another divisive Republican meanie when a statesman was what the party needed. And, of course, it's all on email. One Christie aide wrote, "Time for some traffic problems in Fort Lee," while another responded to news of huge jam-up with, "Is it wrong that I am smiling?"

In a modern scandal, when information, accurate or not, is ubiquitous, we default to shortcuts. Mark Olshaker and John Douglas discuss in their book *Law & Disorder* how it is much easier to believe that the beautiful college student Amanda Knox, convicted of murder while studying abroad in Italy, "was guilty of brutally murdering her roommate [Meredith Kercher] in a frenzy of satanic lust" than it is to believe the less exciting alternative. That alternative is that a young criminal from the Ivory Coast, Rudy Guede, whose DNA was found in Kercher's room and in her body, was her killer. He was convicted of her murder and is currently in prison.

"Foxy Knoxy" was, quite literally, the most attractive suspect available to both the authorities and the international media. Write Olshaker and Douglas, "The beautiful, mercurial Amanda was a defendant almost too good to be true. This was a classic archetypal morality play: Virtue against evil; the good girl against the bad girl. What could have possessed this sultry temptress to kill her equally

Stephen Brashear/Getty Images

lovely friend, enlisting the help of her sexy Italian boyfriend and black African boss. . . . Oh, the powers of seduction this American must have!"

As Errol Morris wrote in his book about the Jeffrey MacDonald "fatal vision" murders, "You can escape from prison, but how do you escape from a convincing story?"

Knox was eventually released on appeal, but the Italian conviction was reinstated in January 2014.

Reputational Cascades

When shortcuts compound during a controversy and contribute to a self-reinforcing crisis, the result is what University of Chicago scholars Timur Kuran and Cass Sunstein identified as "availability" or "reputational cascades." In reputational cascades, the crisis is overdetermined—that is, there are multiple lethal factors at work— and takes on proportions beyond what the raw facts should warrant. Reputational cascades can be good or bad. In politics, strategists such as James Carville, Karl Rove, James A. Baker III, David Plouffe, and David Axelrod have enjoyed positive reputational cascades. In business, Jack Welch and Warren Buffett have benefited from this phenomenon to the point where it is difficult to differentiate between where genius ends and the cascade begins.

The unwarranted hysteria surrounding the chemical agent Alar in the late 1980s, which caused people to discard perfectly safe apples, is an example of a negative reputational cascade. A major environmental group generated the Alar scare and merchandized it with the help of a powerful PR firm, which succeeded in getting support from the likes of *60 Minutes* and actress Meryl Streep.

No one has a formula for the elements that make up a reputational cascade; after all, plenty of events and causes that get media attention fail to snowball. Nevertheless, the overwhelming drive to quickly personify blame, cultural context, and timing are among the elements that drive cascades.

The fate of General Stanley McChrystal, commander of U.S. forces in Afghanistan, is an example of where the velocity of news about alleged insubordination outpaced the cold facts and resulted in his removal from command. As the *New York Times*'s David Carr said in his coverage of the story, "When the mighty fall, the machine goes into overdrive, with different components competing with each other in pursuit of an execution."

McChrystal had given an interview to *Rolling Stone* reporter Michael Hastings where he was alleged to have ridiculed top Obama officials, including the president himself, and suggested that the White House was inept in military matters. Among the tidbits tossed around on cable news and blogs were that Obama was oblivious to warfare and had referred to another general as a "clown." There was also a whiff of racism implied when military brass supposedly mocked the president's name.

McChrystal had been unwise to give the interview, but an examination of his quotes reveals a comparatively boring exchange where he had lamented the length of time it had taken the White House to comment on his war plan and Vice President Joe Biden's penchant for making off-the-wall statements. The more charged comments contained in *Rolling Stone* were actually made by unnamed sources apparently close to the general. This happened over drinks, no less.

Under the convention of "it happened on my watch," McChrystal resigned. These events would have been easier to control in another era when military leaders who got in trouble genuinely *had* said the controversial things they had been accused of. In McChrystal's case, an ill-advised but minor indiscretion was instantly drowned out by blather from anonymous sources and a media environment that disperses what it wants to be true rather than what actually is. The granting of McChrystal's interview may have ignited his scandal, but it was a fuse made of mental shortcuts about loose-cannon generals in unpopular wars that blew him up.

In October 2013, media coverage surrounding an engine fire in the electric Tesla Model S sent the stock of high-flying Tesla Motors down 8 percent. A prominent analyst downgraded the stock from "buy" to "neutral" after the story racked up nearly six hundred Google search hits in a matter of hours (multiplying to about fifty thousand in the following weeks) following a YouTube video of the incident and ominous prognostications about the electric car's future. The *New York Times* referred to the fire as being a potential "stake in the heart of electric vehicles." The drumbeat of negative coverage shaved about $3 billion off the company's market value.

The Tesla incident really happened; the question is the extent to which it was meaningful. There were an estimated 187,000 vehicle fires in nonelectric cars in 2011. Very few (if any) received media coverage. The stock of Tesla, the miracle maker of the wonder car, however, had been up more than 400 percent for the year, which may have contributed to its vulnerability. The same cascade that can deliver saviors can also deliver failures.

Long before Tesla came along, the viability of electric cars had been a subject of contentious debate. Entrenched views about the efficacy of fossil-fuel-powered cars versus the pie-in-the-sky, tree-hugging vibe of electric ones have been congealing for decades. Therefore, when a small negative catalyst entered the scene in the form of Tesla's engine fires, it was framed as an impending disaster as opposed to a statistical possibility. The Tesla fires, therefore, were not really the news; they were only the catalyst that energized an intense cascade that had been gathering for many years.

Scandal and the Role of Timing

Given the power of reputational cascades, the aim of crisis management is to make something bad just a little less bad. The Penn State crisis is an example of where a horrible original sin, the abuse of children by former assistant football coach Jerry Sandusky, was also abetted by snowballing forces.

Among the points of conventional wisdom that arose when the scandal broke was this counterfactual: If Penn State had only reported Sandusky to the authorities when university police first investigated him in 1998 about allegations that he had been showering with young boys, the scandal could have been averted. Turning Sandusky in would have been the morally correct thing to do, not to mention the preferable tactic, but it is naïve to believe the Penn State scandal would have been anything other than a little less bad. Instead of having a gargantuan scandal in 2011, it would have had a merely huge one in 1998.

I assume that the thinking at Penn State in 1998 was that Sandusky would have been "scared straight" by being confronted about the showering incident. Sandusky admitted to showering with the boy, who was a part of his charity devoted to helping troubled children, but he denied that any sexual activity had occurred. Sandusky retired from Penn State shortly after this. His departure would have, in theory, confined a potential scandal, which it did for just over a decade. Nevertheless, Sandusky retained his university privileges and continued abusing boys at school facilities after his retirement. This allowed a reservoir of ill will to gather that culminated with the reputational cascade that broke open when Sandusky was formally charged with forty counts of child molestation in November 2011.

The Penn State disaster represented a moral failing and crisis, but the external variable of timing also affected its scale. Coach Joe Paterno died of cancer in January 2012, two months after the scandal broke. He had received much of the blame during those two months. Had Paterno died, say, a few months *before* the November 2011 revelations about Sandusky surfaced, his reputation would have been grazed but not likely destroyed.

Why? Because when the story broke, the justifiable outrage needed to find a receptacle. This receptacle had to come in the form of a "most punishable party," whose humiliation could be savored by the public in some kind of degradation ceremony. It would have been very hard to place that blame on a beloved legend who had died. The outrage directed against Paterno would have likely fallen far short of triggering the removal of his statue at Beaver Stadium—largely because of the variable of timing.

Penn State has resolved one of the roughly thirty lawsuits that have been filed against the university and agreed to a $59.7 million settlement with the abuse victims.

Think about the role that timing played in the life and career of Congressman Gary Condit, who was widely—and wrongly—suspected in the murder of his former intern Chandra Levy in Washington, D.C., in 2001. In the weeks leading up to the 9/11 terror attacks, the Condit affair was the lead story every night on the cable TV programs. The Internet was ablaze with theories about how Condit had allegedly pulled off the murder, which cross-pollinated into network, cable, and print media outlets.

A few nights before 9/11, I was discussing the damage control aspects of the Condit case on MSNBC's *Hardball* with my co-panelist, attorney Barbara Olson. After the show, Barbara and I commiserated about the absurd proportions to which the Condit case had exploded. She said, "It'll take something pretty big to knock this nonsense out of the news." We made a lighthearted pact to stop talking about the case.

Barbara and I fulfilled our pact but not voluntarily. She was killed on the plane that hit the Pentagon on 9/11, and Gary Condit fell off the face of the earth.

Had the menu of hard news been a little denser in those days, Chandra Levy's murder might never have been laid at the feet of Gary Condit. It may have been more appropriately linked to the rapist-killer who had been prowling Rock Creek Park during that period, and who was eventually convicted of the crime. Nevertheless, at the height of the speculation, true-crime writer Dominick Dunne trafficked in a rumor that Condit had arranged for allies in the Saudi embassy to kidnap and kill a pregnant Chandra Levy. Condit sued Dunne, who ultimately apologized, but in the meantime, this nonsensical theory received a lot of media coverage.

Was Gary Condit an adulterer with a glass jaw? Yes, but he was innocent of murder and very, very guilty of terrible timing. His career got the death penalty.

Witchy Woman

Mental shortcuts played a role in Martha Stewart's insider trading scandal. During an episode in our economy when hundreds of billions of dollars were vanishing in the implosions of Enron, WorldCom, Adelphia, and Tyco, why was Stewart's $45,000 inside tip the subject of far greater media coverage? There were a number of factors that the media and public alike could easily grasp.

Unlike Enron and the other mega-collapses, Stewart was a retail celebrity. Everybody knew who she was. Prior to the scandals, the names Kenneth Lay (Enron), Jeffrey Skilling (Enron), Bernard Ebbers (WorldCom), John Rigas (Adelphia), and Dennis Kozlowski (Tyco) were known primarily to those who read business publications or annual reports. Martha Stewart appeared on the covers of countless consumer magazines and was famous enough to be parodied on *Saturday Night Live*.

Stewart also led a jet-set lifestyle and was widely associated with perfection. The punch line of the *Saturday Night Live* sketches tied back to the flawlessness of every aspect of her life. The term "billionaire" had been injected into the lexicon surrounding Stewart.

Stewart's core violation was also easy to understand: an ultra-privileged person who got an inside tip from another Hamptons socialite and then lied about it. This certified the mental shortcut that the rich are crooked, and that the only way to make it in America is to cheat.

Another shortcut is the double standard that works against scandalized *women*. Having worked with both men and women in crises, I've found that men in trouble tend to be seen as dudes being dudes. Men are scamps, but at some level they are expected to be. Women who get in trouble are framed as being unstable. There is also the subtext of what the British call "getting above one's self": *THIS is what happens when you try to play with the big boys, young lady....* The thinking evidenced here was exemplified during the Salem Witch Trials, when in times of economic uncertainty women were targeted as purveyors of sorcery. *If only they would just behave....*

Taken all together, there was an acute sense of schadenfreude (enjoying the misfortune of others) in watching someone like Stewart not only crash but go to prison.

While Stewart deserved punishment, the media and public reaction to her deeds was disproportional given the colossal financial crimes unraveling at the same time. Her sins of law were middling, but one would think that her sins of cultural resonance bordered on wartime atrocities. Stewart was forced to step down as CEO of her company, Martha Stewart Living Omnimedia, as well as from the board of the New York Stock Exchange.

At the time of her troubles, Stewart's crisis management was criticized even though there were very competent people on the case. In a CBS interview, she was asked about the scandal, and she responded, "I just want to focus on my salad." Media experts insisted that she needed to apologize and hold more comprehensive interviews. The problem with this was that apologies are admissible in court: Given that her position was that she was not guilty, how could she apologize for something that her attorneys were arguing she did not do? As for the expectation that she should conduct a media road show, it had been talking too much (to the authorities) that got her in trouble in the first place.

When Stewart emerged from prison after a six-month incarceration, her damage control was declared a masterpiece. But how could Stewart have been both a crisis management dolt and a savant at the same time?

Neither characterization was correct.

Her redemption was engineered more by the judicial system than anything she did of her own volition. Once Stewart was released from prison, it was having served her time that inspired a sense of public forgiveness, especially among her core audience: women who felt she had been railroaded in the first place. What were people going to say after her prison stint? *Well, she should have been executed.* There was simply nowhere else for the story to go in its natural life cycle but back upward. Stewart never did apologize.

Mental shortcuts catalyzed the witch-hunt spirit of both Stewart's fall and rise: the simple notions that 1) corrupt rich people must be punished in the town square, and 2) people who have redeemable qualities and *are* appropriately punished should be given another chance. The long-simmering counternarrative that the legal and media assault on Stewart had been overkill also facilitated her second chance.

Stewart's brand has enjoyed an impressive recovery. Her goods are sold in Home Depot and Staples, to name a few. Nevertheless, it is unlikely that her enterprise will ever achieve the multibillion-dollar promise it once held.

"It could've taken down the brand. It did not," Stewart said of her conviction years later. "But I must tell you that rebuilding is a lot harder than building."

Randomness Multiplies Shortcuts

Great successes and great failures alike contain an element of randomness that contributes to reputational cascades and their outcomes: The timing of Gary Condit and Joe Paterno's crises, Amanda Knox's beauty, Paula Deen getting sued, Tiger Woods's wife discovering his texts to girlfriends, Lee Harvey Oswald's happening to work in a tower along President Kennedy's recently announced motorcade route (and being a failed communist revolutionary and marksman), Bill Clinton's unlikable adversaries, Bernard Madoff's fraud colliding with the financial crisis that forced his investors to need their money, an unskilled burglar leaving the duct tape on a stairwell door in the Watergate complex, the era in which the Tylenol cyanide tampering occurred, and that a spurned young woman would trigger the unraveling of the Jack Abramoff lobbying scandal by reporting his suspicious dealings to authorities are all examples of serendipity.

These things certainly intersected with human behaviors, skills, and frailties, but they were materially determined by coincidental or invisible factors. In the Twitter cycle, volatility and randomness reign, and it is impossible to determine when the ghost in the machine will collide with an incendiary catalyst or agenda. How do we explain why long-festering grievances exploded into the 2011 "Arab Spring," beyond simply attributing it to Twitter and Facebook? Who could have predicted that after years of low-level rumblings about the appropriateness of the Washington Redskins' team name, in the fall of 2013, the president of the United States would uncork a cascade of outrage in the news media to change it?*
I have been dumbfounded in my own work when trivial gaps in the

---

* President Obama raised concerns about the team name in a televised interview with the Associated Press.

efficacy of a pharmaceutical product snowball into a marketplace crisis, or, conversely, when foreign hackers penetrate U.S. military databases and it receives comparatively little media interest.

For these reasons, it is difficult to set guidelines about when to recall a product, when to preempt a news catalyst, when to respond to one (and how), when to modify potentially controversial policies or behaviors, and when to do nothing at all.

Reputational cascades can affect people who are far less powerful than Joe Paterno or Martha Stewart. Todd Hoffner was the division-winning head coach who planned to spend his career at Minnesota State Mankato until he was ruined by false allegations of child pornography. In August 2012, Hoffner was escorted off the football field where he was supervising his team's practice. He wasn't told why, but he was banned from university grounds.

After going home, and shaking and vomiting in terror, he soon learned the reason. Hoffner was arrested for taking videos with his cell phone of his own children playing. He was charged with child pornography. In some of the scenes, the kids were apparently jumping around, playing naked, after bathing.* In the video, Hoffner's little boy apparently found his private parts to be amusing.

Later, after the children were interviewed and it became clear that they were perplexed by any suggestion that their father, whom they adored, had done anything wrong, a judge dismissed the charges against Hoffner. Nevertheless, he was fired from his job and shunned in his Minnesota community.

The provenance and timing of this tragedy are telling. It began when Hoffner turned his university cell phone in to be repaired. A school employee tasked with fixing the phone noticed the recording and reported him to school authorities. There can be little doubt

---

* The actual videotape was never made public.

that the university was sensitive to child abuse charges the year after the Sandusky scandal broke, which was still in the news.

Following acute controversies, people and institutions that share basic features with those implicated in other scandals become targets of witch hunts that are as equally rooted in the fear of covering one's own bureaucratic hide as they are in justice. The immediate instinct is to punish the first person who trips an alarm, a charge that is often picked up with zeal by prosecutors and the news media.

I have worked on many cases where principals get caught up in scandals simply because they possess similarities to bad actors in the news. The syllogism works like this: IF Sandusky was a college football coach and a child molester AND Hoffner is a football coach, THEN Hoffner must be a similar scourge. Similarly, IF whistle-blowers at Penn State didn't do enough about Sandusky AND it blew up on Penn State AND staff at Minnesota State Mankato have suspicions about Hoffner, THEN taking action against him will best protect the university and their careers. Similar logic occurs among police and prosecutors.

This syllogism may not be enough to convict someone in a court of law, but it is enough to ruin their lives. In such viral ecosystems, there is no difference between suspicion and guilt. Suspicion *is* guilt. The drive toward blame overwhelms everything else, and the cascade proceeds from that. Whistle-blowers, bureaucracies, and the community *know* that the targets are dirty, and if they're not guilty of this particular offense, then they're certainly guilty of something else.

Setting aside the hothouse environment, think about the quotidian aspects of raising young children in the context of the Hoffner case. Children take baths. Parents take pictures of kids in baths. Kids splash around. They jump around naked and have been known to find certain body parts hilarious.

Trouble comes with a confluence of factors: A preexisting, bona fide scandal; hostile players with an agenda; and a cell phone camera that a parent used to record his children playing.

When I first read about the Hoffner story, I thought of the role that technology played in this awful affair. One wonders, if a university associate had simply seen a *paper* photograph of Hoffner's children splashing about, would the reaction have been the same? For years, my grandparents had a picture of "the grandchildren" as toddlers in a bath on their wall. I've seen similar photos in lots of homes. Or is it possible that some of the concerns about Hoffner's "producing" pornography was tied to the fact that he had used his cell phone camera, which could have suggested to his critics an intention to replicate the images for some untoward purpose? We'll never know which factors played what roles in the chain reaction that led to Hoffner's ruin, but the capacity for replication remains a dominant current in the Fiasco Vortex.

More Begets More

The more we hear about a scandal, the more we want to hear even *more* about it, at least for a while.

During the spring 2010 oil spill, BP was hobbled by a more-begets-more syndrome. The primary driver of news coverage was the visual horror of what was happening in the Gulf of Mexico. Particularly problematic was the camera at the bottom of the sea, which belonged to BP, capturing in real time the geyser of oil spewing from the earth. The relentless production of optics coincided with the relentless production of news. There was a direct correlation between the successful plugging of the leak, the halt of the oil-gushing footage from the ocean floor, and the recession of the terrible coverage.

When the Toyota "sudden acceleration" crisis ignited in 2009, each new wave of coverage begat a new wave of consumer complaints, which begat a new cascade of coverage, and so on. A *Harvard Business Review* study of news coverage showed that 106 of the 108 articles the *Wall Street Journal* wrote about Toyota were negative.

Car and Driver magazine calculated that the chance of being killed in a Toyota affected by the recalls was one in 200,000, as opposed to one in 8,000 in any car driven in the United States. Still, the mass psychology fueling the Toyota controversy overwhelmed dry data. The popular blog The Truth About Cars wrote, "The media and 'celebrities are making hay over the Toyota recall issue, desperate to find evidence of electronic and software gremlins.... And there may well be genuine electronic glitches out there, but we'd like to see solid evidence of them. Instead we're stuck with listening to Steve Wozniak's [cofounder of Apple] experience with a faulty cruise control on his Prius. It's being spun as an example of Toyota's electronics Gremlins, creating confusion and scare-mongering. As if there wasn't enough of that already."

In a story about the Toyota recalls, the *Atlantic* reported that a prominent Toyota specialist "faults a runaway media fueled by plaintiffs lawyers, and government regulators succumbing to political pressure. He denies that Toyota had or has any unusual quality problems and sees Toyota's primary failing as one of communication during the unintended acceleration crisis." I agree with this assessment but would replace the word "communication" with "mass psychology" because, as we've seen, "good communication" is not scandal penicillin.

Compounding Recalls

A similar syndrome was at work during the spate of recalls that Johnson & Johnson endured from 2009 to 2012. In 2013, the company agreed to pay at least $2.5 billion to settle lawsuits associated with its hip implants. The recalls, numbering about thirty, involved products such as Motrin, Tylenol, Zyrtec, Rolaids, and Mylanta, and affected eight separate businesses and have cost the company more than $1 billion in charges and lost sales. The reasons for the recalls included diverse complaints such as metallic bits found in products, offensive odors, and inaccurate labeling. The events led to relentless media coverage, congressional hearings, grand jury subpoenas, facility closings, targeting by consumer and environmental NGOs, a sharp stock drop, and the resignations of the company's CEO and the consumer group chief.

Shortcuts metastasized, reinforcing the idea that there was a worm in the J&J apple. It became difficult to distinguish between recalls based in hazards, those initiated due to upgraded manufacturing standards, and recalls that may have been done simply because of the PR consequences of not recalling the products.

How does a company celebrated for its impeccable consumer concern have dozens of recalls in such a short time frame? There are three possible explanations: 1) The company suffered a wave of quality-control problems for which it bore some responsibility, 2) the threshold for recalls has changed on both a regulatory and media scrutiny level, and/or 3) the benchmark of the company's perfection in recent years was set unrealistically high.

The answer combines all three. J&J was candid in its public statements about its need to improve its quality control and apologized for the inconvenience to consumers. In addition, the standards for manufacturing, recalling, packaging, and labeling products, both self-imposed and imposed by the government, have become more strict. The FDA now has the discretion to determine if a company is "in control" of its manufacturing processes, which means both the government and companies are hypersensitive to even the most microscopic particles adulterating products. What's more, science can now detect adulteration in increments that would have been impossible during the days of the Tylenol poisonings of 1982.

Companies like J&J are extremely sensitive not only to government oversight but to the human and brand consequences of even *perceiving* to be unresponsive to consumer safety. The interplay of manufacturing shortcomings, aggressive government oversight, and vigilant self-regulation had a cascading effect on the cluster of recalls. Once the company began recalling products, the operating environment added pressure to recall others. After all, if the company recalled Product A because of reports of a foul odor, how could it, in this pressure cooker, *not* recall Product B after receiving similar complaints?

The mythology surrounding the Tylenol cyanide case established a false baseline for J&J's corporate performance not only because the reality of the case had been distorted in cultural memory, but because the company is operating in a climate that barely resembles the prevailing conditions in 1982. This created an exaggerated contrast between J&J's earlier management and its more recent one: The old guys were wizards, and the newer guys were incompetent.

It's unfair to reach such polarized conclusions about J&J's leadership, but mythology begets mythology, and more than one J&J executive has privately conceded that it's time to retire the legends of the past and deal with the conditions of the present.

Saturation and Desensitization

Exotic behavior is scandalous, familiar behavior isn't. The catch is that, over time, exotic behavior can become familiar and, therefore, less explosive. In Old Hollywood, the classic nightmare scenario for an actor would have been the publicizing of sexually compromising photos. Whereas the proverbial "sex tape" was once a career ender, these days it's a brand extension. Heiress Paris Hilton and celebrity-without-portfolio Kim Kardashian were *made* by their sex tapes. A wholesome teenage starlet seeking to make the transition to adult sensation can load the dice in her favor by lurching in the direction of pornography in the manner of Miley Cyrus's "twerking" at the MTV Video Music Awards.

Desensitization also defines how we view drug use. Supreme Court nominee Judge Douglas Ginsburg was forced to withdraw from contention in 1986 after admitting to having tried marijuana in his youth. A few years later, Bill Clinton's presidential campaign was sidelined, but not destroyed, when the candidate admitted to having tried pot, famously equivocating that he "didn't inhale." While George W. Bush didn't offer a list of drugs he had experimented with, in a subsequent campaign cycle, he admitted to having had substance abuse problems and is widely assumed to have used marijuana and other drugs. By the time Barack Obama ran for president, there were actual photos of him smoking pot, which barely registered as an issue during his two successful campaigns.

Politicians routinely survive divorces and affairs, where they were once career suicide. Gary Hart's candidacy imploded in 1986 when his affairs became public, while Bill Clinton withstood adultery charges during his campaign and presidency. Plagiarism ended the journalism careers of Jayson Blair of the *New York Times* and Stephen Glass of the *New Republic*. A few years later, author Jonah Lehrer, who was caught fabricating quotations used in his phenomenological books, won a lucrative new book contract soon after his scandal erupted.

The challenge for scandal figures is that they cannot fast-forward the acceptance time for culturally sanctioned behaviors; they can only lay the groundwork for future offenders.

More Information Can Be Less Comforting

When managing modern scandals, the more you talk, the more it can trigger additional scrutiny. In January 2013, Notre Dame linebacker Manti Te'o, who had claimed to have lost his girlfriend to leukemia months before, found himself at the center of a scandal when it was reported that this girlfriend did not exist. His relationship with "her" turned out to be by telephone and computer; they had not met face-to-face. The girlfriend turned out to be a male friend "catfishing" Te'o. Every time Te'o gave an interview to explain himself, he said something that introduced a new morsel into the story, which triggered another wave of interest.

Te'o and other scandal principals who have talked too much were doing what felt right on a therapeutic level and what they were led to believe was right on a strategic level. They were wrong.

More information often breeds desperation, not insight. An avalanche of data is confusing so we default to our lizard instinct, which is to distrust the avalanche as the trick of unscrupulous players trained in the art of deception. The Snowden/NSA affair is a case in point: The public claims to want both the protection of spy agencies and greater transparency, however, when we obtain more data, we find it upsetting.

The same holds true with health data. We want more information about the side effects of various medications, but the result is darkly comic advertising that lists every conceivable side effect, however remote. The public has the right to the data it needs to make informed decisions about vital issues, but not all targets of attack should assume that absolute disclosure would be welcomed, let alone forgiven.

During the 2000 election, when candidate George W. Bush was hammered about rumors of hard drug use in his past, pundits called for him to fess up. He limited his public commentary to his past struggles with alcohol, something he was pointedly forced to do when, on the eve of Election Day, a past DUI arrest surfaced. Outside of vague allusions to a reckless past, he never elaborated on his alleged drug use. The drug story died. Had Bush gone into chapter and verse about narcotics, which likely had some basis in fact, he may have offended the Republican Party base and lost the nomination.

Contrast this with Bill Clinton's earlier admission that he had smoked marijuana, adding the flourish that he did not inhale. This level of improbable granularity dogged Clinton's campaign and remained a trope throughout his presidency and beyond.

Swift, decisive actions—firings, confessions, policy changes—don't relieve pressure the way they used to. Gone are the days where "getting it all out there" leads to catharsis. In the period that preceded the Fiasco Vortex, if an organization fired a controversial official, it was likely to defuse tensions because the media, being finite, stopped covering it. Today, if our hypothetical official were fired, the Fiasco Vortex would feature coverage declaring the decision to be a debacle and report on his replacement's shortcomings.

Scandal principals that depend upon public goodwill often must communicate by the very nature of their enterprise. Total silence in the spirit of auto mogul Henry Ford's "never complain, never explain" is rarely an option, but the choice is seldom between all or none; it can be calibrated—and should be.

When the *Costa Concordia* capsized off the Italian coast in 2012, there were calls for the CEO of the parent company, Carnival Corporation, to conduct a media tour. Why would it have been a good idea for Carnival to publicly associate its brand with the deadly disaster? The two cruise lines were not widely linked in public opinion. The subsidiary company, Costa Crociere, rightly oversaw communications associated with the tragedy.

If mental shortcuts are the prism through which we view

scandal, situational variables, as we will now see, determine which ones become blockbusters and which ones flop.

> **Takeaway:** Mass audiences think in terms of familiar stories that tap into deeply ingrained biases and beliefs. These preexisting sentiments are the prism through which people judge new scandals, which compound to create a bigger mess than there would have been otherwise. Human beings are not unbiased data processors. Crisis management is storytelling, but in response to cascading stories, there is rarely a correlation between the greater quantity of communication and vindication. Never underestimate the value of knowing when to shut up or at least focus communications.

12

The Ingredients of Scandal

"I've never had a problem with drugs. I've had problems with the police."

—KEITH RICHARDS

ot all scandals are created equal. Some are worse than others, some catch on, while others don't. There are a handful of variables that affect who and what becomes a target, which targets survive and thrive, and which do not.

1. Bad Facts

Even in a culture where hard facts aren't needed to spark scandal, some semblance of proof ensures a better chance that it will accelerate. Lawyers like to use the term "bad facts" to describe a challenging case. A videotape that recorded a bank robbery and captured the suspect's face is a bad fact. The integrity of an authentic videotape is perfect, as opposed to, say, an informant with a criminal record testifying that a suspect seemed like the kind of guy who might rob a bank.

In early 2013, the media began to examine a variety of allegations against New Jersey U.S. senator Robert Menendez, including those that he patronized underage prostitutes and inappropriately intervened in a federal investigation of a donor, a prominent eye doctor. The media firestorm was intense for weeks but fell off sharply. The reason: There was a huge gap between the spectacle of what Menendez was alleged to have done and the provable facts to support them. One of the alleged "escorts" later admitted to having been paid to fabricate the sex allegations against Menendez and, in fact, said that she had never even met him. A Florida grand jury concluded there was too little evidence with which to indict Menendez on the prostitution charges, but investigations related to using his influence on behalf of a donor remain.

With most lasting scandals there is evidence. In this case, there has been a lot of smoke but no demonstrable fire on the most salacious charges.

A subtheme of "bad facts" is the extent to which allegations are exotic. Politicians embroiled in sex scandals were once a big deal, as were divorce and prior drug use. These days, sexually questionable behavior is increasingly familiar—and decreasingly a career ender, especially in cases when the allegations go unproven.

2. Harm

The degree of injury matters enormously in a controversy's resonance. A president who uses his vast power to punish his political enemies (Nixon) will be seen as worse than one who lies about an extramarital affair (Clinton).

A product that is recalled because of the free-floating possibility that it could be a hazard has a better chance of surviving a controversy than one that has been credibly proven to have killed people.

3. Victims

Who was hurt by the principal? Do we sympathize with them?

The most resonant victims are always children. No one wants

to be in a position where they appear to be hedging or justifying injuries to children and other vulnerable populations.

Helplessness, real or manufactured, appeals to humanity on a visceral level. One need not be an animal rights activist to be sickened by the sight of ducks in the Gulf of Mexico struggling in vain to stay afloat while weighted down with the soup of oil from the BP blowout. When seeing people whose livelihoods were destroyed by the oil spill, we empathize with them if for no other reason than our projected horror over being in that same position.

One of the reasons it is harder to win popular support for a war than it used to be is that technology allows us to see what war looks like unedited. Images of the maimed and dead cancel out romantic notions of valor and heroism.

4. Motivated Adversaries

One of the first things I consider when I get a new case is, who is the client up against? Some enemies are more formidable than others. Facing a stalker-blogger isn't fun, but going up against a still-mighty media organization and congressional investigators is worse. The Susan G. Komen foundation learned this when it came up against the abortion rights movement after it defunded Planned Parenthood's mammogram program. Planned Parenthood has a passionate constituency and a powerful organization to support it.

While the theoretical power of the "far right" frightens a lot of people, when it comes to organizing boycotts and affecting consumer behavior, I have found that its influence pales in comparison to what more progressive groups can do. A main reason for this is that big retailers and consumer products companies recognize that mainstream media organizations will position the initiatives of conservative groups as being driven by moral superiority or hatred while progressive forces square with media notions of tolerance.

In public, corporate PR staffs maintain the party line that their responses to boycotts and product "de-selection" (deciding not to make or sell a particular product) are based upon sound science. In private, however, the very suggestion of a boycott by an activist group with media savvy will trigger contemplation of pulling a product from the shelves in order to avoid a prolonged battle or embarrassing loss.

Examples of direct and indirect de-selection campaigns anchored more in the fear of antagonists than hazard include: retailers banning the plasticizers bisphenol A (BPA) and phthalates; formaldehyde, which in minute amounts prevents the growth of bacteria in personal care products; phase-outs of the antimicrobial agent triclosan by retailers and consumer products companies; bovine growth hormone rBST; and polystyrene packaging despite ample evidence that alternative packaging is not more environmentally sound.

Cowards! some say of surrendering companies, but wait: If you are Wal-Mart, with obligations to your shareholders and employees, is it in your interest to go to war to keep a particular shampoo on your shelves because you believe so passionately in the active ingredient? If you are a consumer products behemoth with hundreds or thousands of brands, is it worth spending millions of dollars to defend a cleaning agent that goes into .001 percent of your products or just phase it out and be done with it? If you are the CEO of a manufacturing conglomerate with tens of billions in revenue, is it easier to go to war with a minority group leader claiming systemic corporate bigotry or cut his organization a check for a hundred thousand dollars, which you'll earn back in a fraction of the time it takes an autopen to sign the name of the company treasurer?

Issue-driven activists understand this dynamic. Just as a mutual fund picks stocks to buy, NGOs pick products and companies to attack, boycott, and legislate against, hoping for a payoff. Sometimes they identify worthwhile targets, but when there's rent to pay, notoriety to achieve, regulators to befriend, and state attorneys general to cultivate, sometimes you need to produce a sequel to whatever outrage launched your NGO in the first place.

For the targeted company, it comes down to a cost-benefit analysis. Is the fight worth it? If you're McDonald's, and you sell hamburgers, it's hard to strike a deal with animal rights activists to stop slaughtering cows. But if you're McDonald's, and environmentalists are ransacking your restaurants because you sell those hamburgers in polystyrene "clamshells," it's not as hard to get rid of the plastic packaging, which is what McDonald's did when the pressure got too intense.

As these cost-benefit analyses are conducted, the prospect of a handful of moms on Facebook boycotting your business is increasingly considered a serious risk.

What kind of resources do the controversy's originators and protagonists have? In the Herbalife case, the company was facing down billionaire hedge fund managers with teams of influential media consultants—good reasons to take this threat seriously. Groups devoted to animal rights and the environment have vast budgets with which to attack their targets; their targets, meanwhile, often need to go to boards for approval for even the most modest defensive budgets.

Who is rooting for the crisis creator? Movies and television shows almost always portray plaintiffs' lawyers in a positive light. The opposite is true of big businesses. One of my favorite faux articles from the *Onion* is entitled "I Just Love Corporations," where the author lists the companies she likes as if they were baseball players or rock stars. Despite the sermons of corporate chiefs about the good they do and jobs they provide, consumer activist Ralph Nader and the late Mike Wallace of *60 Minutes* made more compelling figures to believe in because they were ostensibly representing our interests against ogres angling to hurt us.

Woody Allen's ongoing travails exemplify the sheer willpower of some motivated adversaries. More than two decades after his ex-partner, Mia Farrow, accused him of molesting their daughter Dylan during a bitter breakup, the allegations resurfaced when Dylan, twenty-eight, wrote a piece in the *New York Times* restating them with great force and color. Never mind that the claims had been investigated and rejected long ago by the proper authorities: All it took to relight this fire was Dylan, likely with maternal encouragement, to *decide* to re-publicize the charges. The ostensible news hook here was the Academy Award nominations associated with Allen's film *Blue Jasmine*. Allen's only recourse was to again deny the claims—thereby repeating them—which he did in the *Times*.

The sheer power of Allen's celebrity, the universal horror of child molestation, and the natural constituency of abuse victims assured Allen's conviction by hashtag.

To empathize with Allen's predicament put his constituency in the position of appearing to defend child molestation at worst, and doubting Dylan, surely a victim (of *something*) in distress, at best. Who wants to take that position at a neighborhood barbecue?

5. Constituents

Those who survive controversies usually have constituents invested in their survival. The principal isn't in the fight alone. Martha Stewart benefited from the loyalty of women consumers, many of whom believed that she had been excessively punished. Apple Computer consistently wins consumer support in circumstances when other companies would not. Toyota's and Tesla's resilience was tied to the long-standing loyalty of their customer bases. A North Carolina State University analysis showed that, "[d]espite the high-profile media coverage of the Toyota recalls, there was very little effect on what consumers were willing to pay for a Toyota."

Specific brands inspire loyalty, not companies. Some of this may be because people don't like change and often look for excuses to embrace familiar things.

In times of crisis, is anybody really rooting for the corporation outside of its employees and investors? Corporations rarely have constituencies. Employees and shareholders are natural allies, but even these stakeholders assume that the company is powerful enough to do what has to be done without them having to volunteer for additional service.

I knew that Bill Clinton would survive the Lewinsky scandal when women—the cohort most likely to be offended by his sexual behavior—rallied behind him, token comments about "not defending what he did" notwithstanding. Sometimes a fight comes down less to "who do we like" and instead "who do we hate more."

Clinton was blessed by his adversaries. In Cliff Jackson, a fellow Arkansan who had attended Oxford with Clinton, the president had a nemesis who was widely perceived as a bitter rival envious of his ascendency. Jackson had played a role in mobilizing Arkansas state troopers to allege that they had set up sexual trysts for Clinton while insisting, "It has nothing to do with sex...sex is a symptom of the basic Bill Clinton—the deception, manipulation and exploitation of people."

In Whitewater prosecutor Kenneth Starr, there was a widespread feeling that Starr was a puritan relic investigating Clinton's sex life versus "high crimes." No matter how many times Starr's team and Clinton's critics asserted that the investigation wasn't "about sex," this point failed to resonate. It didn't help that Clinton's alleged misdeeds associated with the original Whitewater land deal in Arkansas were so confusing that they vanished from the public debate.

Natural alliances can rarely be manufactured, only exploited. Clinton mobilized a campaign to discredit his critics, but nobody was being fooled in the process: Women's support of Clinton was organic, as was the broader and visceral discomfort with a special prosecutor examining presidential sex, a topic that many people found entertaining but not worthy of removal from office.

Phil Robertson, the *Duck Dynasty* patriarch, survived his suspension after making controversial remarks about gay lifestyles largely because he had a solid base of viewers that delivered very strong ratings. These viewers believed Robertson was getting railroaded for simply expressing religious views that were politically incorrect; they were not going to be easily moved from this position the way diverse consumers of an auto company might be. Robertson was also a known quantity: Few among his core audience could have been shocked by his views.

When quick-service food chain Chick-fil-A CEO Dan Cathy expressed opposition to same-sex marriage in 2012, San Francisco, Chicago, and Boston leaders said they would ban the company from their cities. Corporate partners such as the Jim Henson Company, producer of the Muppets, ended its partnership. Despite many protests from the gay community, sales at the restaurants sharply increased. Many supporters of the Georgia-based company, which has a committed following in the South, felt that the protests against Chick-fil-A violated the company's freedom of religious expression. Even though Chick-fil-A ceased donating to certain organizations that opposed same-sex marriage, the company's hard-core constituency had buoyed the chain during the most challenging moments of its controversy.

6. Hypocrisy

Hypocrisy—posing as being one thing but being the opposite— is one of the great catalysts of outrage, one that may explain the unique revilement of former senator and vice presidential candidate John Edwards.

Edwards's spectacular fall from grace also contained incendiary variables. He didn't just cheat on his wife. Edwards cheated on his *dying* wife, who had been canonized in the news media; did so during a presidential campaign; had a baby out of wedlock with his mistress; lied directly, unequivocally, and on camera about the affair; and cooked up a whopper of a story, whereby he enlisted an aide to claim paternity.

Much of Edwards's equity was cinematic: He was the quintessential John Hughes movie good guy, the prom king who chose the plain girl. Elizabeth was not just a candidate's spouse; she was the central pillar of his persona. It was Elizabeth who made Edwards more than just another haircut, which many people suspected was all he was in the first place. The couple had even lost a child and endured. This was real love, certified by gaudily renewed wedding vows. Elizabeth's aura *was* John's substance. If he had her, there must be something under all that hair.

When Edwards was caught running from the press in a Los Angeles hotel while visiting his illegitimate child and mistress, it was akin to the first tile flying off the space shuttle: One comes off at great speed, and then they all fly off. Edwards's betrayals were fundamental to what we had come to believe about him, as opposed to being collateral to his perceived nature. Everybody knew who and what Bill Clinton was and thought they knew who Edwards was. When Clinton lied, Americans said, "well, yeah," but when Edwards did, he told us that we were all morons. *World-class* morons who were dumb enough to fall for his renewed wedding vows and his New Age mistress with whom he had become acquainted when she served as his campaign videographer. And with whom he had even made a sex tape (which against all odds was destroyed before it went public).

People who merchandize their perfect lives have the glassiest jaws. We take an interest in them because we know our own lives are so flawed. Unlike the Edwardses, time and tragedy don't make us stronger and bring us closer together; they make us weaker and drive us apart. We wanted to watch them tumble down the stairs and end up on their rears like the rest of us.

Elizabeth's illness exempted her from this schadenfreude, which is why it all fell on John. Just as blame must find a deserving host, it must also bypass the sanctified. Illness and death have the effect of benediction, and Elizabeth's role in this mess is one few have the appetite to explore.

Why does hypocrisy bother people so much? After all, most people understand that many of us fail to meet our high standards. The answer lies in the insult, the deceiver believing that the deceived is not only unworthy of the truth but too stupid to detect the lie.

Edwards was a character firmly anchored in his own cosmetics. From his obsession with his hair (disturbingly captured on a YouTube video to the tune of "I Feel Pretty") to his moist-eyed antipoverty crusade, despite living in a 28,000-square-foot mansion, the only thing that seemed plausibly real about him was his long marriage.

When it turned out that Edwards had been cheating on his terminally ill wife, it was too much to forgive.

7. Operatic Personalities

A prosecutor friend once lightheartedly told me that he liked going after gangsters with the most colorful nicknames. This applies to controversies, too, since both the media and consumers of scandal are as attracted to "big" personalities as crows are to shiny objects.

New York governor Eliot Spitzer had built his career on scorched-earth takedowns of high-profile corporate targets as state attorney general. And some lower-profile ones, too: Spitzer had gone after prostitution rings. With Spitzer, there were never mitigating circumstances, just Good versus Evil. Spitzer was the Good in this formula, so what could be more fun than watching his jaw shatter when he was the one who delivered the haymaker to his own face by consorting with prostitutes.

Paula Deen was not only a huge personality; she was an archetype from another era—an unabashedly southern woman who promoted foods that are now accepted as being unhealthy.

When she admitted to having used a bigoted epithet, it tapped into our greatest national drama: race. The spectacle of race combined with Deen's persona overwhelmed any contextual issues such as the vintage of her remarks and the conditions in which she made them.

The travails of the Los Angeles Dodgers became tabloid fodder when the then-owners, Frank and Jamie McCourt, endured a bitter divorce, including Frank's firing of Jamie from the team. Their lifestyle, which included $74 million in home purchases and a $12 million swimming pool, kept the drama in the news for longer than was good for any of the parties.

It is impossible to recall the Tyco corporate scandal without referencing CEO Dennis Kozlowski's $6,000 shower curtain (for his maid), $15,000 umbrella stand, and the over-the-top birthday party he threw for his wife, which featured an ice sculpture of Michelangelo's David urinating vodka.

8. Likability

Some crisis principals are more likable or, at least, supportable than others. Apple Computer violated many crisis management conventions under Steve Jobs's reign, and few people cared. In the age of transparency, Jobs dissembled about his poor health with few consequences—because consumers love Apple products. Another company would have been eviscerated. In the age of the-customer-is-always-right, when a new iPhone had an antenna problem, customers were basically told they didn't know how to hold a phone correctly, and blowback was limited—because consumers love Apple products (the company wisely introduced a corrective modification "bumper"). In an environment where "empowerment" and philanthropic self-promotion reigns, Jobs was abusive to colleagues and famously averse to charity, all with minimal blowback—because consumers love Apple products.

Scandal doesn't stick to investor Warren Buffett in part because he gets results and people like him. In 2011, Berkshire Hathaway executive David Sokol, who many thought might succeed Buffett, recommended a chemical company he had invested in, Lubrizol, as a takeover target to Buffett. When this surfaced, Sokol resigned due to the possibility that his activities could be seen as insider trading. It was a big story for a few days, but it disappeared quickly. That the Securities and Exchange Commission (SEC) decided not to take the matter up as an insider trading case doesn't explain why Buffett wasn't hurt more. Investigations are dropped and defendants are acquitted a lot, and scandal figures remain tainted.

Some read sinister doings into Buffett's lack of trouble in the Sokol affair, as if he held sway over the SEC and the news media. It's possible that business news outlets may have been reluctant to lose their biggest interview guest but not likely. The media love to hunt for big game. The explanation might be something much more banal: Perhaps the folksy Buffett is just not someone people are especially excited about attacking.

President Reagan benefited from his likability. Friends who worked for Democratic legislators on Capitol Hill, and who disliked Reagan, were convinced that the White House media operation shifted into damage control mode whenever Reagan committed one of his gaffes. I remember one friend asking me as a young White House staffer, "What do you tell the press when Reagan says something like 'trees cause pollution'?" I answered, "We say, 'he says stuff like that.'"

The rules of engagement work differently depending upon who is under attack. A study of the Romney campaign's communications failings, as reported by the *New York Times*, concluded that "Mitt Romney's campaign never came to terms with the new dynamic. Instead, his organization responded with a defensive crouch that fenced off the candidate from the very people he needed to reach."

Also, "the Obama campaign did a much better job of adapting to those realities than the Republican opponent."

This conclusion is absurd. Few leaders hold the media at a greater distance than Barack Obama, a strategy that has accrued to his benefit throughout his career. Like Reagan, Obama is a "big arena" player; he talks over the press not with them. Why would Romney, whom most of the media detested, have fared better had he communicated more with the press? He wouldn't have: The media by and large liked Obama and supported his ascendance and disliked and/or did not wish to promote Romney's bid for office.

When President Obama was contemplating using military force against Syria over its use of chemical weapons against its own people, questions arose about the palpable lack of pacifistic protest from Hollywood over Obama's intentions. Actor/activist Ed Asner explained to the *Hollywood Reporter*, "A lot of people don't want to appear anti-black by being opposed to Obama." This explanation gets to one of the most volatile variables in crisis management: Much of what detonates as an issue is affected by how crisis creators feel about who the controversy will blow up *on*. Sometimes, likability and political supportability are interchangeable.

When navigating controversies, a benchmark is needed to establish what vital audiences think of the principal to begin with. Beloved technology or consumer product companies will be treated more gently than "dirty" industries like petrochemicals or firearms. It is no accident that the bookends of 1980s crisis management involved Johnson & Johnson (Tylenol tampering, 1982), a company that made cuddly products such as baby shampoo and baby powder, and Exxon (*Exxon Valdez* oil spill, 1989), a company that drilled Mother Earth for nasty, polluting oil. This contrast helped frame the distorted notions of what we consider good and bad crisis management.

9. Optics/Memes

Big scandals contain symbolic "optics"—iconic videos, photographs, documents, emails, flashy sound bites. Think about: the bloody glove, wailing Akita, bleached blond houseguest Kato Kaelin, and White Ford Bronco (O. J. Simpson trial); fake trading floor (Enron); blue dress and cigar (Clinton-Lewinsky scandal); "wide stance" in an airport restroom stall (Senator Larry Craig); "Mission Accomplished" banner (Bush's premature declaration of the end of combat operations in Iraq); videotape of beatings (Rodney King and the Los Angeles riots); emails referring to gullible clients as "muppets" and the CEO's characterization of investment banking as "doing God's work" (Goldman Sachs); emails referring to Indian clients as "f-ing monkeys" and "troglodytes" (Abramoff lobbying scandal); deposition acknowledging racial epithets (Paula Deen); radio broadcast referring to Rutgers women's basketball team as "nappy-headed hos" (Don Imus); disparaging quotes in *Rolling Stone* about superiors (General Stanley McChrystal); crotch photos and tweets and the nickname "Carlos Danger" (Anthony Weiner); telltale email correspondence and readily available photos of glamorous biographer-mistress Paula Broadwell (General David Petraeus); televised testimony of distressed victims of "sudden acceleration" (Toyota); photos and film of capsized ship, stranded passengers (Carnival Corporation); video footage of oil spewing from ocean floor, and vast pollution, and the CEO's "I want my life back" comment (BP); videotape about 47 percent of Americans unwilling to take personal responsibility (Romney campaign); the candidate screaming (Howard Dean campaign).

Never mind that some of these items were tweeted and distorted beyond the realm of context; that's precisely the point. The role of optics is to serve as emotional validation of a bias not to educate or clarify.

In 2013, People for the Ethical Treatment of Animals released a distressing video depicting a worker at a rabbit farm in China tearing the fur from a screaming rabbit that would ultimately be used to make angora sweaters. PETA called upon prominent retailers to cease using angora in their products. Even though not all rabbit fur is sourced in this inhumane manner, many retailers agreed to phase out angora. In this campaign, the visual and audio display of suffering was what drove it toward its outcome.

Inversely, the allegations surrounding Senator Robert Menendez were unaccompanied by optics. Had there been photos of him with underage prostitutes, the sexual aspect of his scandal may have metastasized. No one produced any such evidence. Had George W. Bush's cocaine use allegations been accompanied by attendant photos, he might never have been president. Alas, no photos, just gossip from sketchy characters.

10. Controversy Congestion

Much of what becomes a scandal is determined by what else is happening in the cultural, business, and political climate. The recession of 2001 triggered outrage over corporate collapses of this period. Anger over the failure to find weapons of mass destruction in Iraq exacerbated notions of the Bush administration's vast, dark powers, which inspired investigations on multiple fronts, including: the politicization of prosecutorial appointments in the Department of Justice; the congressional scandals involving lobbyist Jack Abramoff; lawsuits and congressional hearings involving private military contractors; and the legal machinations associated with the exposure of CIA operative Valerie Plame, whose husband, former ambassador Joseph Wilson, disputed the Bush administration's contention that Iraq was seeking to obtain materials to build a nuclear weapon.

Had Bill Clinton had an affair during a recession, the country may have reacted more angrily than it did. *What's he doing messing around with a young girl when the country is going down the tubes?* Rather, the Lewinsky scandal occurred during a period of peace and extreme prosperity.

The zeal to investigate a company that has lost investor money will be more intense than the zeal to investigate one that has made investors rich, independent of the methods that led to these outcomes. While the Enron scandal wave was gaining strength, unjustifiable subprime loans and other instruments were making big money, but no one cared, until consumers began defaulting on loans years later.

11. Resources

One of the most important determinants of who survives crises is the resources the principal has to fight back with. Companies such as Toyota, News Corporation, and Johnson & Johnson overcame their challenges in part because they had the resources to battle major antagonists such as plaintiffs' lawyers, competitors, and the federal government.

A company like Goldman Sachs had the resources and political muscle but not the cultural and media alignment to win popularity beyond that. Goldman survived (and prospered) during the Great Recession, investigations, and lawsuits, but the bank won't win any popularity contests.

Susan G. Komen and Livestrong were in very different situations. Even if Komen had decided to stand by its position to defund mammograms with Planned Parenthood, it would have had to justify using charity money to underwrite the battle. If Livestrong had decided that Lance Armstrong's contributions to cancer research and awareness warranted his remaining at the foundation he created, the organization would have had to justify using limited resources for this purpose. Instead, Livestrong parted ways with Armstrong.

Negotiating the conditions highlighted in this chapter requires us to differentiate between things that are done in the full view of the public and things that are handled more discreetly. Next we'll begin to redefine "winning" and "losing" in crises by surveying the "Controversy Iceberg" that distinguishes between above- and below-the-surface navigation techniques.

> **Takeaway:** As some illnesses are more serious than others, some controversies are harder to negotiate. There are a handful of variables beyond command-and-control "handling" that determine how a crisis is likely to play out. By reviewing the conditions in this chapter, you may be able to help determine how serious a crisis is—or is not—and what actions are called for to navigate it.

REDEFINING WHAT
IT MEANS TO WIN

13

The Controversy "Iceberg"

"There is no section in the *New York Times* recording the stories of
those who committed crimes but have not been caught."
—NASSIM NICHOLAS TALEB

I think of a controversy as an iceberg. There is a small tip that
the world sees and an enormous mass below the surface that
makes up the bulk and essence of the enterprise. In other words,
most of what's really happening is happening in a place that few
people see.

The above-the-waterline elements of crisis management that
people see are the TV interviews, the apologies, the product recalls.
Then there is what the public doesn't see—behind-the-scenes conflict avoidance, operational and strategic maneuvers, offering
choices, working with regulators, and deal cutting. What remains
unseen is often more important than what *is* seen, and the best
damage control efforts are often resolved discreetly.

Notions of what constitutes good damage control are biased
against "silent evidence," techniques that are boring and discreet,
and even unpleasant. Business schools rarely teach case studies
about those that avoided problems by keeping their heads down or

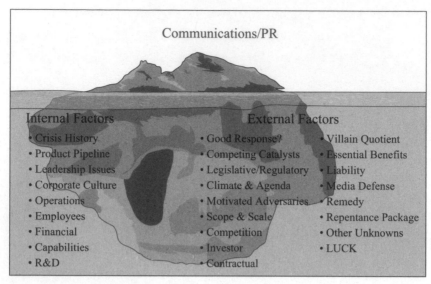

Communications/PR

Internal Factors
- Crisis History
- Product Pipeline
- Leadership Issues
- Corporate Culture
- Operations
- Employees
- Financial
- Capabilities
- R&D

External Factors
- Good Response?
- Competing Catalysts
- Legislative/Regulatory
- Climate & Agenda
- Motivated Adversaries
- Scope & Scale
- Competition
- Investor
- Contractual

- Villain Quotient
- Essential Benefits
- Liability
- Media Defense
- Remedy
- Repentance Package
- Other Unknowns
- LUCK

Crisis Management Iceberg

muddled through controversy by settling lawsuits and withdrawing from controversial businesses and practices. The soft drink industry has navigated nutritional minefields by acquiring water and juice brands and offering caffeine-free alternatives. Celebrities stop doing drugs, politicians with secrets choose not to run for office, and shareholder concerns are allayed through executive charm offensives rather than on Twitter.

When Merck faced lawsuits over its arthritis drug Vioxx, analysts estimated litigation would cost the company a staggering $25–50 billion. Conventional wisdom said to apologize, settle, and undertake a reputational improvement campaign, especially since Merck's stock was trimmed by a quarter of its value upon its announcement of Vioxx's removal from the marketplace in 2004. The company instead decided to fight the lawsuits. Merck's initial forays in court were not successful, but the company believed its legal position was strong, and persisted.

Eventually, the court cases began going Merck's way, and the company reached a $5 billion class-action settlement in 2007. In most circumstances, this wouldn't be considered good news, but in comparison to *what could have happened*, it was certainly "less bad news." Merck had decided that the defense of its reputation was better determined by a below-the-surface campaign to demonstrate the venal nature of the lawsuits than by embarking on a vague image campaign that would have failed to undo the damage. You will read very little in the damage control canon praising Merck's work on this case.

We celebrate that Johnson & Johnson apologized and recalled Tylenol during the 1982 cyanide crisis, but rarely discussed are the hundreds of millions of dollars in settlements the company paid to victims. The Tylenol case was celebrated because it *ended well* for Johnson & Johnson. This "hindsight bias" attributed the successful *outcome* of this case to the company's flawless management of it. It ended well, therefore it was well managed.

Herbalife's battle with short sellers began to turn when billionaire backers Carl Icahn and Daniel Loeb entered the fight on its behalf, contingencies that became public but began behind closed doors. There is nothing like powerful and well-financed angel investors to turn the tide.

The role of the scorched-earth tactics that the Clinton administration deployed against its adversaries during the Lewinsky scandal doesn't make for a comfortable lecture in a college civics class. It's far more convenient to offer the post-Watergate saw that the cover-up is worse than the crime. Clinton's defense was not a cover-up as much as it was a sub rosa counteroffensive aimed at his critics that exposed these critics' vulnerabilities.

Toyota and the Dividends of Preaching to the Choir

Toyota entered the Fiasco Vortex in 2009 when off-duty California Highway Patrol officer Mark Saylor and three family members were killed when his Lexus sedan (a Toyota brand) accelerated, crashed through a fence and a dirt berm, and ended up in a river. The central allegations were that an engine defect caused Toyotas to spontaneously accelerate and that applying the brake would not halt this acceleration.

Toyota ceased all sales in the United States, a highly unusual move. The recalls, which covered accelerator pedals, poorly aligned floor mats, and other braking issues, ultimately involved nine million cars. The company lost $2 billion in sales and spent $1.1 billion to settle individual lawsuits, plus another $1.6 billion to settle class-action claims associated with the loss in value of customers' cars. This does not include the billions spent on the operational costs of the recalls themselves.

All of this played out in exhaustive news coverage, cable punditry, and congressional hearings, where the CEO of the company apologized.

The Toyota story began to turn around at about the time allegations surfaced about the questionable claims of some of the plaintiffs. There was the widely covered case of James Sikes, who alleged that his Prius had accelerated to nearly 100 miles per hour in California until a police car had to forcibly stop it. Sikes demanded a new car as part of a proposed settlement with Toyota. There were problems with Sikes, however, and his story triggered interest due to his enjoyment of the media spotlight. It turned out he owed $19,000 in car payments and was in debt to the tune of $700,000. He had also been accused in the past of filing false police reports, in addition to fraud and theft. A review of the technical aspects of Sikes's claims confirmed the implausibility of his story.

Examinations by the National Aeronautics and Space Administration (NASA) and others rejected the allegations that Toyota engines were causing the vehicles to spontaneously accelerate, but the news surrounding this vindication on the most serious charges was a blip in the media vortex. In coverage of one particularly notorious incident, the *Los Angeles Times* didn't even report that the driver of a runaway Toyota had been indicted for being under the influence of marijuana and vehicular manslaughter.

A few weeks after NASA's report was released, I asked a room filled with one hundred business leaders from around the world how many of them had known about Toyota's recalls. Every hand went up. When I asked how many were aware of NASA's exculpation report, only three or four had heard the news.

I do not know the extent to which Toyota encouraged the examination of its detractors, but this exposure promoted a counternarrative that gave permission to loyal Toyota owners to keep their faith that something other than "sudden acceleration" was at work here.

This counternarrative is an example of managing the below-the-surface elements of the crisis iceberg. This means introducing or promoting arguments that trigger a revisiting of the dominant story line in a way that is not visible to the public.

Said Secretary of Transportation Ray LaHood, "We enlisted the best and brightest engineers to study Toyota's electronic systems, and the verdict is in. There is no electronics-based cause for unintended high-speed acceleration in Toyotas."

Why didn't Toyota tout its vindication? After all, if the company had been wrongly accused, why wouldn't its leadership shout this from the rooftops? Because doing so would have reignited the controversy at a time when the brand was regaining consumer confidence. Realizing that a hostile media doesn't profit from vindication, publicity would have given a platform to legitimately grieving people, plaintiffs' lawyers trolling for clients, know-nothing pundits, consumer advocates, government officials calling for further investigations, not to mention sparking a new wave of me-too claims from disgruntled drivers.

Similarly, Procter & Gamble didn't pound its chest after a court smacked down the class-action attorneys suing them over the Pampers Dry Max shakedown referenced in the "Brittle" chapter. The company wisely let the story die and let the product's robust sales do the talking. Once you escape from a whirlpool, why would you want to go back and splash around in it?

Unsurprisingly, Toyota's critics didn't buy the NASA vindication. The watchdog group the Center for Auto Safety claimed NASA's investigation wasn't thorough and demanded greater rigor. To what end, one wonders? Until the *right* investigation draws the *right* conclusions, I suppose. Wrote *Fortune*, "The word of the rocket scientists apparently wasn't good enough."

Playing Through the Rough

The Tiger Woods case was another example of where the best crisis management happened below the surface. There was one person who could have made the scandal considerably worse: Tiger's wife, Elin Nordegren. Elin, along with her children, could have appeared on multiple television shows and posed for magazine covers rehashing her feelings of betrayal. The psychic injury to the children would have become an entire spinoff of the crisis. This would have inflamed the already terrible coverage Tiger was getting, not to mention his personal recovery. Such interviews and appearances never happened. Some of this was because Elin was not instinctively drawn toward the limelight. But strategic discretion also played a role: Clearheaded parties, including the scandal's principals, recognized that certain things were best resolved off camera.

And, to a large degree, they were. Tiger and Elin came to a divorce settlement with little fanfare. Tiger lost his endorsements with Accenture, Gatorade, AT&T, and *Golf Digest* and did not win contract renewals with Tag Heuer, Gillette, and Buick. In 2010, the year following the crisis catalyst, he lost an estimated $22 million in endorsement income. He kept endorsements with Electronic Arts (video games), NetJets, and Nike, and he won endorsements with Rolex and Fuse Sports.

The much-speculated-upon legal charges associated with domestic violence (potentially for both parties) evaporated entirely. Had Tiger and Elin spoken about the explosive night in November that led to his car crash, it could have detonated a whole new level of heartache for the couple, their children, and his career. Instead, Tiger was charged with careless driving, fined $164, and given four points on his license. Since Tiger is worth hundreds of millions, he could handle the fine. All in all, an excellent result considering what could be achieved below the iceberg's waterline.

There were a few public actions, however. While pundits were demanding a Tiger media tour, he issued a simple public statement acknowledging the "embarrassing" incident, and he thanked his wife for acting "courageously." A few months later, he made a public apology at a tightly controlled press availability but did not take questions. The apology was criticized, but as we've seen, the "botched apology" punditry is an inevitable part of the Fiasco Vortex. The subject faded from the news, which was the real objective—not impressing people with the eloquence of the apology. I know at least one corporate sponsor who made a hand-washing gesture, as if to say, *And now we can all move on.* This sponsor did not fire Tiger.

In July 2013, *Forbes* magazine placed Tiger number one on its list of top-earning athletes with total prize and endorsement income of $78 million. Interestingly, he never dropped off the list post-scandal; he just went down a few places. He also collected six tournament wins in a twelve-month period. Among his most lucrative endorsements was from stalwart Nike, which launched an advertising campaign in 2013 with the tagline, "Winning takes care of everything." Some were offended by this theme, given the scandal three years earlier, but the tagline was an apt clinical summary of a remarkable recovery given the abruptness and speed of Tiger's derailment.

The Nike tagline's boast about sports victories as a crisis management strategy spoke volumes, but it is silent on some vital points. Tiger, like Kobe Bryant before him, committed a sin *that had nothing to do with his core specialty*, unlike Lance Armstrong, whose very athletic excellence was corrupted by his secret steroid use. The ability to exercise one's unblemished core talent must play the lead role in redemption because victory is only meaningful if it's authentic.

Under the Sea

A noteworthy example of a below-the-surface crisis management resolution, quite literally, involves the BP oil spill. For eighty-seven days, the Fiasco Vortex whipped BP for mismanaging the spill, often mistaking the crisis for the crisis management. Some of the more amusing commentary seemed to suggest that if the company had just used Twitter and other communications with greater savvy, perhaps the whole thing would have gone a little better....

There was a direct correlation between the plugging of the leak and the end of the acute phase of hostile coverage. *This was an operational achievement*, complicated by the BP camera on the ocean floor that recorded every drop of oil belching from the earth.

Once the leak was sealed, BP could undertake other critical below-the-surface initiatives such as cleanup, preventative improvements, and compensation of injured parties.

BP, chastened from the oil spill and its green-washing "Beyond Petroleum" image campaign, took a more focused approach to its post-spill above-the-surface communications. In the spring of 2013, the company launched a newspaper advertising campaign about its lawsuit settlements. The ad took direct aim at the potential billions that plaintiffs' lawyers stood to earn from the oil spill's settlements

Who's benefiting from the Gulf Settlement Agreement? The numbers tell the story.

Three years ago, BP made a commitment to the Gulf, and every day since, we've worked hard to keep it. As part of that commitment, we entered into a settlement agreement designed to help people and businesses that suffered losses from the spill. But that agreement is now being misinterpreted to allow payments to businesses for losses that did not occur and do not exist.

Some plaintiffs' lawyers are now attacking BP for identifying serious problems with the interpretation of the agreement. They say it's working "exactly" as it should. That's not surprising – the facts show that the lawyers defending this flawed interpretation are also some of its biggest beneficiaries.

- Law firm claimants have received more in offers from the Court Supervised Settlement Program (CSSP) than restaurants, bars, hotels, or seafood processors. The average offer made to law firms since the start of the settlement program is **$812,000** – more than three times the average offer made to all other businesses.

- The average offer made to law firm claimants has more than doubled in size since the end of May, to more than **$1.5 million** per claim. And law firm claimants have already been offered almost **$250 million** overall from the CSSP. One of the firms on the court-appointed committee leading the litigation against BP, as well as individual partners in another committee law firm, have even filed business economic loss claims for themselves.

- These enormous payouts are on top of the generous fees that law firms are already earning for representing businesses and individuals with economic loss claims. In fact, lawyers are taking up to **25%** of the compensation their clients are awarded by the settlement program. And with over **$4 billion** awarded to claimants thus far, that means law firms could stand to collect more than **$1 billion** in fees.

- Under the settlement agreement, the lead plaintiffs' lawyers also could share up to **$600 million** for negotiating the deal and representing the class.

Whatever you think about BP, we can all agree that it's wrong for anyone to take money they don't deserve. And it's unfair to all the honest, hard-working people of the Gulf for this settlement to be a boondoggle for plaintiffs' lawyers.

To date, BP has spent $14 billion on response and cleanup to help restore the Gulf environment. We've paid an additional $11 billion in claims to help restore the economy. And we remain committed to paying every legitimate claim from anyone who suffered real financial losses.

bp

BP

at the expense of their clients, for whom the suits were filed. The message: BP will only settle legitimate claims that benefit the true victims of the 2010 disaster.

In a case like this, the legal and PR battles are ongoing, so reminding the public about the disaster was less of an issue because it will be in the public sphere regardless.

Do targeted campaigns like this improve BP's image? Not really, but they do introduce risk to those who pursue frivolous claims or don't truly benefit injured parties. Aggrieved class-action plaintiffs will pay attention because they are the ones who have lost so much and are motivated to win redress. BP's advertisement gives the plaintiffs an action they can take—demand fair play from their lawyers on class-action settlements—rather than attempting to make a large and diffuse population feel tingly about an oil company, which goes against how normal people are hardwired to feel about energy behemoths.

Redemption Through Deft Business Moves

Netflix is another company that found its redemption below the surface of the crisis iceberg. In July 2011, Netflix announced a sweeping change in its movie and TV show rental business. Instead of continuing with its $10 per month flat fee for "streaming" *and* DVD delivery, the company decided to charge $7.99 for streaming and another $7.99 for DVD delivery. This forced subscribers who wanted to keep both services to pay a 60 percent price increase and manage two usernames, two payments, and two different websites.

Netflix lost 800,000 subscribers in the months following its ill-fated announcement, and its stock fell 80 percent by year end to around $60. The company correctly predicted that 2012 would be a money loser because of the turmoil. Two months after its initial announcement, Netflix CEO Reed Hastings apologized for the price increase and for separating the streaming and mail services.

Despite the missteps of 2011, the company had a comeback plan. Hastings bet heavily on its "streaming" capability and allowed it to cannibalize its once-thriving DVD market. Netflix DVD services remained, but the focus—even with narrower margins—was on streaming. Netflix also expanded internationally and invested in original content, producing the Kevin Spacey political series, *House of Cards*, which won three Emmys. By October 2013, Netflix had 40 million subscribers, more than HBO, which had a decades-long head start. At this writing, the company's stock is trading at all-time highs around $350, up more than 500 percent from its 2012 low. An improved business model controlled the damage and allowed Netflix to prosper.

Letting the Law Take the Lead

My firm was retained by a prominent figure at a well-known institution. I'll call him Bill. A woman with whom he had had an extramarital relationship had become embittered by his ending of the affair and decided to seek revenge. I'll call her Mimi. She began to allege malfeasance on Bill's part at that institution. With the help of a small cabal of plotters, Mimi threatened to go public with spurious claims unless Bill, who was wealthy, paid her an exorbitant sum of money.

This sounded a lot like extortion—in the true criminal sense— to Bill, his lawyer, and me. Mimi was threatening to destroy Bill's career, his family, and his life by falsely alleging that he had committed crimes unless he paid her millions of dollars. Incredibly, the PR people at Bill's organization said he should publicly apologize for the relationship. I was stunned by this leap toward the clichéd apology.

"Apologize? She is threatening to accuse him of committing felonies that he didn't commit!" I said.

"But he did have an improper relationship," the PR man said. "He needs to ask forgiveness."

"Perhaps from his wife," I said. "But if the cops think there's a case here, playing offense is better. Once Bill is cast as a trapped fox, this will be the story line for eternity. His guilt for committing a crime, which he didn't, will be implied. If he did one sketchy thing, he did them all. That's how people think."

We agreed to approach law enforcement. Bill's lawyers called the police, who believed they had a case of conspiracy to commit extortion on their hands. Mimi and others were successfully prosecuted. Bill acknowledged his relationship with her, but he was never associated with malfeasance, which was the greater concern.

All of this begs the question: *Why not just pay Mimi off?* After all, there are many occasions where I have advised quiet settlements.

Following were the variables we had to consider:

1. Money. The amount Mimi wanted was outrageous. Paying it would have financially crippled Bill despite his success.
2. Crime. We correctly believed that Mimi had committed a crime. We weren't talking about a garden-variety civil shakedown.
3. Discretion. Accusing a well-known figure of a serious, career-ending crime is not the kind of thing one hushes up these days. Not only did we not want to cover it up; the best option, given the situation, was to publicize it with our characterization once news coverage was inevitable.
4. Volatility. Mimi was crazy, and she wanted to be famous. You can't sign nondisclosure agreements with somebody who wants to be Lady Gaga because she would have taken the money, gone public anyway, and then come back for more.

Whether mitigating exercises are found below or above the surface, they are not the exclusive province of professionals. Just as controversy can envelop ordinary people who are just living their lives, as we wrap up, we'll see that these same people can negotiate many big challenges with good judgment.

> **Takeaway:** Most crises that are successfully resolved are resolved due to business and operational considerations, which occur beneath the surface of the controversy iceberg. Because these actions are often mundane and invisible, they go unheralded. Above-the-surface communications strategies are overhyped as damage control solutions, which may play a supporting role, but shouldn't divert attention away from the big decisions that will ultimately determine the health of the principal.

14

Fewer Gurus, More Grown-ups

"The dogmas of the quiet past, are inadequate to the stormy present. The occasion is piled high with difficulty, and we must rise with the occasion. As our case is new, so we must think anew and act anew. We must disenthrall ourselves, and then we shall save our country."

—ABRAHAM LINCOLN

As I hope this book has demonstrated, I believe we place too much faith in gurus who claim to have answers to complex situations, especially reputational crises. I would take it a step further and suggest that those with life experience and good judgment can take a punch better than the self-styled experts who populate the landscape.

Whether a crisis principal is a multinational company or a private citizen, the current cultural and technological climate has rendered reputations uniquely fragile. If our collective jaws are more brittle, what's a potential principal of a controversy to do? Part of this book's message has been to recognize that every scandal is its own animal and that there is no definitive playbook. Achievable expectations and "grown-up" good judgment defuse more controversies than quaint gospel and yield the touchstones of advice that follow.

Everyday Good Judgment

From time to time, friends and acquaintances will ask me how to manage challenges associated with their own reputations. Many of these people are decent, hardworking souls who don't run conglomerates or have platinum-selling albums. Let me offer a few examples of challenges they've faced and how I advised them.

A friend I'll call Nancy was confronting rumors that her small graphic arts business was successful because of an affair she was alleged to have had with a prominent client. The rumors were false and were being fueled by competitors, something familiar to women who are both successful and attractive. She wanted to deny the charges in correspondence to customers. I thought this was a bad idea.

"How many of these people do you think actually have heard this rumor?" I asked.

"A lot," Nancy said.

"Perhaps, but is it possible that you are so upset by this that you are assuming that other people are thinking about this as intensely as you are?"

Nancy acknowledged that possibility but was adamant about defending herself. I understood her feelings. To me, the issue wasn't whether she should defend herself, but how—and at what volume.

"Don't you think that people hear rumors like this all the time and don't give them much thought? And, assuming the rumors were true, don't you think if customers like your work, this will be the key factor in their decisions to hire you?" Finally, I asked, "Are you more concerned about potential customers or existing ones?"

Nancy acknowledged that not everyone listens to rumors and that existing customers would be less affected by gossip than future ones. We agreed that future customers would be the focus of any outreach. Nevertheless, we couldn't do anything that would draw unwanted attention to her problem among those who may never have heard the affair stories.

We rejected the idea of any broad-based communications. Since much of Nancy's business was word of mouth, we focused on a *few* people who she was almost certain had already heard the gossip and had also served as references for her work. Nancy approached a select few customers, inquired about their awareness of the rumors, and asked them to kindly let her business prospects know that they were false—on a reactive basis; that is, only if the subject was brought up. This cautious approach was the better of her mediocre options.

At the same time, Nancy increased the showcasing of her graphics work in promotional materials, including online, so that her work would play a more prominent role than her appearance or personality. While the latter were undoubtedly assets, in the context of the gossip, they were also potential liabilities.

While we never could measure the effectiveness of this strategy, in time the salacious stories receded, and her business was successful.

Another friend, David, authored a blog post that was critical of a prominent and controversial figure. In the piece, David made ill-advised reference to the individual's oversized personality, lifestyle, and, well, size. We'll call the big shot Falstaff.

Falstaff went public with a letter to David's employer, who suspended him. Falstaff also threatened to have David fired from his day job by alleging he was an insensitive loose cannon who was likely to get his employer sued.

When David came to me for advice, one thing was clear: He had to apologize, and he had to mean it. He prepared an "open letter" apology to Falstaff, which was published on his blog. At the same time, we launched an effort to find people who could get to Falstaff. I wanted David to reach out to Falstaff and meet with him. I had no illusions that the two would reach any kind of agreement on the core issues or develop a friendship. My mission was very narrow: to prevent Falstaff from taking any further steps to ruin David. Falstaff was the far more powerful man in this situation, and if he could be reminded of the differences in their status, I thought it would have a chilling effect on his behavior. Moreover, Falstaff was very sensitive to how he was publicly perceived.

David made a concerted effort to meet with Falstaff. When they met, David again apologized without equivocation or rationalization. He told Falstaff a little about himself, including how angry his family had been at him for the mean-spirited blog post. Falstaff had been lukewarm during the meeting, but there were no further acts of retribution. David was eventually reinstated at his job. He makes it a point to have a colleague check his blog articles before he posts them.

As we've seen in this book, I take a very skeptical view of rigid crisis management ground rules, whether they apply to powerful organizations or ordinary people. Nevertheless, in the conversations I have with people like Nancy and David, who face more workaday challenges, I find myself making common points time and again. They are:

1. Don't mistake caution for paranoia. Paranoia is an *irrational* fear that people are out to get you. Caution is a rational assessment of your vulnerability, and, on the digital frontier, we are all vulnerable.

2. Regulate social media participation. It's fun, but stimulation shouldn't be mistaken for wise strategic communications. Investigative reporters and other hostile parties use networks like LinkedIn to find people who know you and who may not wish you well. Why make it easy for them to make your life hard?

3. Take a breath before clicking "send." Most communications are instantaneous and cannot be retrieved. Consult a friend

or colleague if you're not sure about how something may be perceived.

4. Consider the necessity of the "Reply All" email function. You probably don't know who "all" consists of and to whom they owe their loyalty. One of them may share your email with someone who can hurt you.

5. Put a small piece of duct tape on your smartphone and computer camera lenses. Put a barrier between yourself and a "selfie"—or a hacker using your lens to spy on you. (Yes, this happens.)

6. Not everybody is happy for you. You may be enjoying your success and your beautiful family, but resentment plays a huge role in provoking attacks. Think carefully about how self-celebration may be received.

7. Don't overrespond. Being attacked in public forums is painful. Nobody handles reputational attacks well. "Thick skin" is a myth. Responding for therapeutic reasons or for vengeance rarely ends well. There is a spectrum of responses that range from declaring war to doing nothing. The best response lies somewhere in between.

8. Beware of reputation defense services. Most of them are confidence snares. If these gimmicks really worked so well, they would be bigger than Apple, and they're not.

Determine the Best *Achievable* Outcome

I always ask clients in crisis what they really want to accomplish. What is their true objective—and the most realistic one, the "best achievable outcome," as communications wise man E. Bruce Harrison has phrased it?

Is the objective truth? Justice? Peace? Money? Vengeance? Self-esteem? To be loved?

In the midst of controversy, the scandalized don't always answer honestly largely because they are not certain. They often claim that truth is the goal, but the pursuit of truth can be fraught with peril. Truth requires an airing of dirty laundry, and few parties are as pristine as they believe they are. This is not to suggest that everyone has a terrible secret, only that in the midst of a firestorm, the smallest infractions are easily framed as big ones. A good drug that can trigger adverse reactions can easily be portrayed as a "bad" drug that kills people. In the Fiasco Vortex, the story is "killer drug," not "drug that helps a lot of sick people but not everybody because a small percentage of people who are already sick will have bad reactions to the most effective drugs."

There is also a tendency to deny the human impulse toward vengeance against one's accusers, when this is often what drives initial crisis management responses. Vengeance, however, is a self-destructive objective, and I'm not in that racket anyway.

A successful survival strategy must be anchored in a clear-headed appreciation of what's doable. While forgiveness and recovery are often achievable, getting people to unknow or unremember a controversy is not.

Surviving a controversy is often a matter of context. Susan G. Komen will survive but may never be as big as it might have been without the Planned Parenthood flap. General Petraeus may still have a lucrative career in business, but he'll never be president. Paula Deen can remain a successful chef, but her universe will contract. Toyota and Netflix survived and prospered, but it took time. These were achievable outcomes.

Who Do You Care About?

There are those whom you may want on your side, but, more important, there are those whom you *need* in order to survive. It's an exercise in masochism to define success by winning over your detractors. It's their job to *not* like what you do. I am amazed by how many huge corporations wring their hands and spend fortunes trying to get their critics to love them. Not all differences are misunderstandings that can be bridged through exchanges of data; many are core conflicts and tribal skirmishes. If victory is measured by converting one's adversaries, failure is certain.

Hitting Back Requires a Weapon

Pushback campaigns require weapons, the basis of which must be a strong counternarrative to prevailing wisdom.

One of the better pushback campaigns in recent memory was Tesla's counterpunch to a negative review of its Model S by the *New York Times*'s John Broder. Broder claimed that the car ran out of energy during a test drive in a cold climate. Tesla's Elon Musk responded by publishing detailed charts on its website of Broder's test drive—the vehicle has a "black box" that records its performance—that claimed to show that Broder had essentially let the car run out of energy by not charging it properly. Both the *Times* and Tesla swatted back and forth at each other over the significance of Tesla's black box data, but the key point is this: Tesla counterpunched by giving its supporters a contrary position to rally behind and forced its critic, the *Times*, to respond to its questionable assertions. Recognizing that it was in this fight long term, there was little risk to Tesla in working to ensure that its position was in the media bloodstream.

Lengthen Your Recovery Time Frame and Redefine Success

Scandal principals have very limited control of their short-term fates in the Fiasco Vortex. You can neither rebuild your house in a hurricane nor judge the long-term health of a patient mid-surgery. You must redefine the tenets and time frame for recovery.

Redefine success on your terms, not those of audiences that will never be satisfied. When a crisis hits, and the media start calling, it's tempting to play Whac-A-Mole and try to satisfy every inquiry at the same time others are popping up. In concept, being responsive is better than the alternative. But when controversies are instantly deemed botched, and calls go out for purges, this can have the unintended effect of sabotaging worthwhile efforts. The fallacy is that the true objective of any crisis is to satisfy the immediate demands of vocal critics—who are often committed to their discontentment—as opposed to the long-term mission of the principal.

Sometimes those who know an enterprise best are uniquely qualified to guide it through crisis. In the autumn of 2013, Secretary of Health and Human Services Kathleen Sebelius came under fire when the website for the new national health-care program experienced multiple glitches. Calls for her resignation and a shutdown of the website arose in multiple corners. President Obama, however, stood by Sebelius.

Why was this smart? The Obama White House clearly appreciated the long-term nature of the "ObamaCare" launch. There was no way that this launch *wasn't* going to have some form of difficulty, predictable or otherwise. To fire Sebelius knowing that problems would remain for a while would have put the administration in the position of having to fire another HHS secretary in short order. This would have made things worse by ushering in a perceived cavalcade of incompetence. Besides, Obama could always fire Sebelius later.

The same holds true for the draconian recommendation at the onset of the crisis that Obama shut down the health-care website for repairs. Taking the site offline would have set expectations that a perfect website would be forthcoming, which the White House knew was impossible.

Also, a mere week prior to the website's launch, it was the Republicans who were on their heels, in the wake of a government shutdown. The news shifts rapidly, so what was the risk of working "below the iceberg" to fix the website's problems rather than provoke more cycles of bad coverage by taking actions that might not pan out? When under attack, you can only work with the earthly options you have, not the divine options you wish you had. The better of Obama's bad options at that time was to buckle in for a rough ride and make decisions on a reality-by-reality basis.

In the short term, few scandal figures fare very well. In the long term, many do. The ones who survive abandon their hopes of *escaping* a scandal and focus instead on *enduring* one.

Stick with Your Nature

On multiple occasions, Barack Obama has been criticized for reacting too calmly to criticism. *"Get mad!"* critics urged when Mitt Romney overwhelmed Obama in the first 2012 presidential debate. The problem with this was that Obama is a calm guy. If he had lost his cool, it would have seemed like a psychotic break or he would have been framed as the "angry black man," a stereotype that he doesn't even remotely resemble. Obama knows precisely when to *not* get mad—or at least conceal it—which has been one of the keys to the success of his political career.

In his 1984 reelection campaign, President Ronald Reagan's staff became concerned that his opponent, the policy-savvy Walter Mondale, would overwhelm Reagan with his mastery of facts, which was never Reagan's strong suit. Accordingly, he was overbriefed with too much data. In his effort to convey expertise, Reagan seemed befuddled. This sent a panic throughout the Reagan campaign. In the next debate, Reagan stuck to big concepts, far fewer facts, and interpersonal warmth. He was reelected by a landslide.

The same idea holds true with organizations as it does with individuals. You cannot take the culture out of an institution; you have to work within the group's constitution. A wholesome Midwestern food company will probably have a very different makeup than a Russian mining company and should make decisions accordingly.

Timing Waves

I've used the symbols of cascades and waves in this book because they are apt metaphors for overdetermined controversies. Prior to the emergence of the Fiasco Vortex, crisis management was anchored in fighting a wave by introducing a contrary argument into the debate. Waves were smaller and shorter back then, so that a fast, good-faith effort could make an impact within a sleepier news cycle.

Today, rapid pushback against troubling allegations is likely to be met with disappointment. Your message is likely to get crushed in the wave regardless of how good you think it is. It doesn't mean you should let falsehoods stand, but the first wave of hostilities may need to wash over you before a counternarrative can emerge. At some point, the seas will calm and become more conducive to a better defense.

There are four ways to handle a big wave: go under it, dive through it, run from it, or ride it. A lot depends on where you happen to be standing and the size and direction of the wave. Sometimes, by keeping your head down, you can avoid getting hit. Martha Stewart valiantly tried to dive through the wave in the early stages of her insider trading scandal. The first wave crushed her but eventually passed. When she emerged from prison, there was nowhere else for the wave to go, so she rode its wake to recovery.

Senator Menendez ran from his wave, and the initial allegations were too weak to catch him.

Toyota was crushed in the early stages of its recall controversy and has reemerged as the top-selling auto manufacturer, reporting a 70 percent profit surge in the autumn of 2013. At this writing, the waves of Johnson & Johnson recalls are most likely in their final stages, and the company has spent its time underwater rebuilding its quality control capability.

Saying No

Pick your battles. Not every cause is worth undertaking. Your objectives should be tied to survival and prosperity, not taking on suicide missions.

I no longer take clients I don't believe I can help. Whereas all criminal defendants benefit from an attorney (if only to protect their rights), not all scandalized principals benefit from a crisis manager.

For example, I have a "no crazy people" rule. Megalomaniacs, drug-addled celebrities, and corrupt organizations that don't think they have a problem may have the right to legal counsel, but they don't have the right to my assistance. They are often beyond advice and counsel. Fatally damaged clients and causes bring everybody down and get you sued, and they often don't even pay.

Before venturing into a crisis management program, consider whether it's a case you can see your way out of once you get in. As Nietzsche wrote, "The value of a thing sometimes does not lie in that which one attains by it, but in what one pays for it—what it costs us."

As with all viruses, one of the best preventative measures is to limit exposure to things that can hurt you. In the early 1980s, Lew Wasserman, the fabled chief of MCA, which owned Universal Studios, had the opportunity to buy the then-distressed Walt Disney Company. MCA's younger staff groused, believing it had been a missed opportunity by an aging mogul who didn't appreciate the opportunities of an acquisitive environment. Wasserman, however, had survived repeated federal government investigations throughout his long career, including alleged antitrust violations, game-show-rigging scandals, and organized crime ties. He had been forced out of the talent agency business altogether. His former client Ronald Reagan was president, and rumors had been hovering for decades that something untoward had occurred when Reagan, as head of the Screen Actors Guild, had given MCA an exemption to be in both the talent and television production businesses.

Wasserman knew that a move on Disney could stir up all the old ugliness and put a target on his back. His younger colleagues had never experienced such existential struggles and couldn't fathom them. By this time in his life, Wasserman knew that he wasn't immortal. He may have missed an opportunity to get bigger, but he averted an opportunity to be destroyed.

That was "getting ahead of the story."

Controlled Venues

One of the most promising aspects of the Internet is that targets of reputational attacks now have outlets that they didn't used to. Whereas mainstream media such as *60 Minutes* were once the alpha and omega of news coverage, attack targets can now choose not to go on the program; instead they go straight to their own websites or YouTube, where they can speak freely without interruption or hostile mischaracterization. The reach and credibility are lower, but so are the chances of self-destruction. Legacy media don't like these alternatives and often decry them as being the wrong strategy, which really means, "Why didn't you let me destroy you during Sweeps [ratings] Week?"

Those who survive within organizations in crisis tend to be

whoever's fault the mess *isn't* perceived to be. This is one reason why people in crisis-consumed outfits are loath to appear on camera, the fear being that the outrage will seek a human symbol. Think JetBlue's David Neeleman and BP's Tony Hayward, both of whom lost their jobs.

It is better to avoid TV interviews where you know your adversary is going to scream at you and cut you off than it is to attempt to paralyze them with your rapier wit. Modern technology provides plenty of alternative options for communications.

Give Somebody Else a Victory

In the first season of *The Sopranos*, Uncle Junior and Tony Soprano are feuding over who will become boss after the death of the reigning North Jersey kingpin. After a period of profound tension, Tony strides into Uncle Junior's place of business and, in front of the older man's crew, embraces him and concedes the position to Junior, who is delighted.

In mid-embrace, as his uncle beams, Tony whispers into his ear a particular union he wants control over as the price for his surrender. *After* he (Tony) concedes, Uncle Junior, suddenly seeing his new victory disperse and fearing a loss of face in front of his men, nods in agreement.

Uncle Junior gets the title and the law enforcement scrutiny that comes with it. Tony gets the power and the money.

When a company has come under fire from critics to cease certain controversial practices, I have advised them when it has been feasible to change that practice—and allow critics to take the credit. It's not a crisis manager's job to be a hotheaded obstructionist; it's to return the client to normalcy. If allowing an external party to claim victory ends the unpleasantness, so what?

Inventory Your Liabilities

It's hard to look at one's own "negatives." We have built in survival mechanisms that urge self-delusion. In Edith Wharton's *The Age of Innocence*, the narrator speculates about why the protagonists proceeded with their misguided affair: "Olenska was like no other woman, he was like no other man: Their situation therefore resembled no one else's; and they were answerable to no tribunal but that of their own judgment."

So it is with many parties that become embroiled in controversy: Driving toward one's destiny, inexorable forward movement, is hardwired into the system. Self-critical feedback loops are not. The problem with the question *What were they thinking?* is that it assumes the behavior in question is an aberration, as opposed to being a side effect of ambition fueled by a little success. The collective wisdom of civilization does not profit its descendants. Pride may precede the fall, but self-exemption precedes scandal. *I am me, therefore that which I do is moral.*

There is a fetish within today's community of overachievers to think of themselves as outlaws, rebels, people who "break the rules." This has become so prevalent that it's an ironic form of conformity, whether it's wearing flip-flops in the office or proselytizing *kumbaya* politics from the safety of a corporate campus. It betrays a central truth amid the self-delusion: The outrageously successful not only believe—but often have actually found in real life—that the laws of the universe really don't apply to them, that is, until they do.

I think back to the hulking boxer from my youth who fell to the smaller man. What had the Hulk been thinking before he climbed into the ring? I imagine that he was consumed with satisfaction over his size and the deference it had afforded him throughout his life; his triumphs over a heavy bag that hadn't hit back; exaggerating the significance of the few fights he had already won; and unable to imagine that such a shrimp could flatten him.

I may have smirked at the Hulk's defeat as a teenager; however, at middle age, I am far less judgmental. Despite my life experience, there is nothing that renders me immune in the wrong circumstances from the same self-deception that felled that giant.

Students and colleagues often ask me, "Do new clients ever come in to you and just say, 'I screwed up'?" Rarely. This is because recognizing one's liabilities is a long-term proposition. *Anagnorisis*, the term in Greek tragedy for the moment in the drama where the protagonist recognizes his seminal flaw and how it contributed to crisis, comes over time and at great cost. The principal is the last one to realize he has a problem. He tends to think that the real issue is a lack of awareness of "all the good I'm doing." This results in such misdirection as indicted corporate chiefs taking minority children to ballgames—tactics that may have a marginal impact at sentencing but rarely affect public opinion. Good works are viewed as things the privileged *should be doing anyway*, not acts that require more rewards than they've already enjoyed in life.

Situational Awareness When It Comes to Discretion

Lecturing people on the importance of discretion is futile. More practical advice is to encourage discretion and security where possible, *but accept the expansion of creeping surveillance as our permanent habitat, and make a few defensive strategic decisions, as opposed to trying to implement futile tactical ones.*

In the same spirit that it is wiser for a recovering alcoholic not to go into bars, it is smarter to assume that unrelenting surveillance is now our natural state. It is easier to have an automatic email scrubbing system than to try to convince people to manually delete old emails. They won't. It is better to block access to social media and porn sites from a corporate office than request that people not access them. They will. It is better not to join social media sites that you won't really use than to join them only to agonize about whether adverse parties are checking you out on LinkedIn. They are.

In my business, I came to find managing rampant leaks at the client level so futile that I ceased taking on certain cases. The leakiest clients turned out to be trade associations or coalitions, which have obligations to multiple members; cases demanding information sharing with several consultants; and celebrity clients with entourages, each member of which has his or her own private set of ambitions and grievances.

Among the most naïve assumptions is that everyone is on the same team. A particular problem is that of the entourage. It is often members of a principal's inner circle who are leaking damaging information. In our celebrity-obsessed climate, those who are part of a principal's posse often think of themselves as the "star." Eventually, there is that moment when the posse member realizes that he's not the star, he's the "help." And that's when he calls Page Six.

The motives for leaks or sabotage from supposedly friendly parties include resentment, spite, strategic differences, or the desire to endear one's self to a reporter, government agency, or watchdog for one's own purposes. As Walter Winchell said, "I usually get my stuff from people who promised somebody else that they would keep it a secret."

Because of strict professional codes, laws, and professional risks, attorneys are less likely to leak than are rank-and-file members of an organization or consultants.

Despite the superficial cloak of privilege, there is a near certainty that any item given to Congress in compliance with a subpoena will be leaked in order to build a media audience for an upcoming hearing and endear the member (or staffer) to the reporter. A congressional subpoena is only a legal inquiry in the sense that it carries the force of law; its real objective is to reward allies and punish targets.

The quickest way to ensure the failure of any program is to leak a strategy memo. Once a game plan is publicized, opponents can beat it, which is the whole point of the leak. It is easy to make the most harmless memo appear sinister through select quotations. One test of a principal's fitness for crisis management is the extent to which they demand detailed written plans. Companies that don't recognize the perils of discovery during litigation and through leaks tend not to have what it takes to weather a scandal.

Be Realistic About Libel Law

Libel law plays less of a role in attacks on the powerful than many think because it is designed to protect the press, not aggrieved targets. The media (and other critics) are legally permitted to be biased, unfair, and even inaccurate. What libel law prohibits is "actual malice," which means that the reporter cannot leave evidence that it is her intention to harm a target. It also prohibits a "reckless disregard for the truth"—a *provable* pattern of aversion to the facts in order to hurt a target. Both of these tenets of libel law are very hard to prove.

Where libel law tends to help is *before* a story ever runs. "Prepublication" strategies of delineating precisely, with the help of counsel, what would be considered false and defamatory if published or broadcast, yields better results than vague threats about suing for libel. It's rare to stop a bad story; it's common to build a hurricane fence around one by making clear in advance what's true and what's not.

One of the best things about the Internet is the emergence of the "media criticism" discipline. Media leaders recognize that biased and uninformed reporting is a threat to their enterprise. They also realize that they are legally protected. Libel law doesn't, however, protect the media from embarrassment, which is where media criticism comes in.

Reporters often claim not to be bothered by what critics say about them. Not true: Most reporters are exquisitely sensitive to criticism, and their editors and producers don't like it very much, either. Many investigative reporters see their roles as nailing bad guys. They convince themselves that their targets are uniquely worthy of destruction and that anything they do in the service of the takedown is virtuous.

Targets of media wrath enjoy First Amendment rights, too, which can be exercised by reaching out—and writing for—diverse media criticism venues including *Buzzfeed, Gawker, Poynter, Newsbusters, Media Matters, Big Journalism, Timeswatch,* and *Mediaite.*

The Authenticity Dare

Somewhere along the line, an expectation emerged that scandal figures act with false panache. This led to one of the more obnoxious devices of my trade, where tarnished public figures stand before cameras with fake smiles declaring that they "welcome" an investigation. Really? Who welcomes an investigation?

I think this silliness goes back to Richard Nixon, who was prone to believing that everything was artifice, thus his sad attempt to be Kennedyesque by walking on the beach...wearing wingtip shoes. While John F. Kennedy advanced his career through the careful merchandizing of his appearance and social skills, what Nixon overlooked was that the image of the martyred president walking on the beach with his two children really was a magnificent sight. That Kennedy exploited this was opportunism, not alchemy.

Americans have elected plenty of leaders without Kennedy's style, including Nixon. While you can't always change your image, you often can get audiences to accept your flaws.

Sometimes authenticity is the best swindle. Ronald Reagan's grandfatherly disregard for details and his penchant for off-the-cuff misstatements were routinely forgiven. Bill Clinton's alley-cat libido made his lying about sex perversely truthful; after all, isn't that what guys like him do?

There is nothing wrong with acknowledging fear and mortification in certain circumstances. One of the most genuine displays of authenticity in recent memory was the impromptu news conference held by Ruslan Tsarnaev, the uncle of Boston Marathon bombers Tamerlan and Dzokhar Tsarnaev, immediately after their identification as suspects. Ruslan called the pair "losers" and said if he had suspected them, he would have turned them in himself. He said, "Of course we're ashamed! I teach my children—and that's what I feel myself—I respect this country, I love this country. This country, which gives [a] chance to everybody else to be treated as a human being...."

This was very different from what Americans had expected from Muslim Americans in the wake of 9/11, when condemnations of the suicide bombers were underwhelming. Ruslan behaved in a manner befitting the man he was: a law-abiding American citizen who valued human life and who cherished the life he had made for himself in the United States. He was visibly shaken, and his mortification differentiated him—and most Muslim Americans who were horrified by the bombing—from the two murderers who were responsible.

Restrained Planning

A ten-page plan is preferable to a hundred-page plan. It's better to focus on the three big things that are most likely to happen than the thirty that probably never will. If given the choice between a detailed plan and strong leadership, focus on leadership.

There are two exceptions to my aversion to overplanning. The first concerns industrial accidents, which involve complicated systems and extensive regulatory compliance. There can be serious consequences for not managing things in a very specific way, and one ignores these requirements at their peril.

Second, resource contact lists—employees, media, customers, vendors—often need to be exhaustive.

The aspects of crisis management that don't lend themselves to overplanning are those that require judgment in rapidly changing circumstances. You can't plan good judgment and good luck. Crisis simulations can help assess vulnerabilities, set priorities, and select spokespersons, but neither vague nor specific plans trump good leadership.

Muddling Through

"Muddling through" is the stepchild strategy of crisis management. Nobody celebrates those who improvise their way through adversity by responding minimally, seeing what turns up, bolstering the support of allies, quietly correcting problems and missteps, and throwing a counterpunch when the opportunity arises.

Winston Churchill, at the depths of his wartime leadership, was unafraid to extol the virtues of muddling through, which he did with cries of "KBO!", an acronym for "Keep buggering on!" As Samuel Beckett starkly wrote in *Waiting for Godot*,

VLADIMIR: What do you do when you fall far from help?
POZZO: We wait till we can get up. Then we go on.

Look to Art, Literature, and History

When young people express interest in going into the crisis management business and ask what they should study, I usually point them to the liberal arts. There is more to be learned about controversy in art, literature, and history than in most graduate management schools because the latter have been corrupted by a very narrow dogma and are platitude factories on the subject of damage control. The arts and history, however, contain many impressions of reality and a diverse array of insights into human behavior.

When I teach graduate business students, we deconstruct real-world cases and discuss what the arts can teach us about damage control. On our reading list is Ernest Hemingway's *The Old Man and the Sea* because the "old man," Santiago, survives to tell his story of survival. That's it. He doesn't kill the sharks or return to shore with his prize marlin.

It is equally important that would-be crisis managers understand the irrational and unfair elements of many scandals. This is why my classes talk about the Old Testament's Book of Jonah, where the eponymous prophet is tossed into the sea by a group of sailors who need to blame a stranger for the sudden and terrible storm they encounter.

Enough with "Closure" Already

My least favorite New Age cliché is "closure." Its implication is one of clear resolution and the peace that theoretically derives from it. I understand its appeal, but does anyone grieving from a loss ever really achieve "closure," or will they simply learn to survive the loss and hope that the intensity of the pain recedes over time?

In most scandals, the intense aspects recede but are rarely resolved in a way that pleases the principal. All of us would like to vanquish our enemies and have the world recognize our unjust treatment; we would also like to have a Greek chorus despise our enemies as much as we do; and we would like people to unremember the bad things that they heard about us.

As the benchmarks for damage control success are established, it's essential to distinguish between what needs to be accomplished versus what the principals wish to accomplish. Closure is overexpected and underachieved.

What Would Jackie Do?

A key risk factor for becoming a target of attack lies in our culture's mania for publicity. We increasingly measure our worth by our visibility. Is it any wonder that both General David Petraeus and Senator John Edwards, no dummies, were seduced into self-destruction by their chroniclers?

In the Fiasco Vortex there is no greater perceived failure than to *not* be a "brand." But must everybody be one? (Dare to entertain the horrifying possibility that you might *not* be a brand.)

I have been in hundreds of meetings about reputational issues where the alpha man or woman presiding said "this is not about getting better publicity for me," which means precisely its opposite.

Setting aside the strategic role publicity provides in many ventures, there are plenty of people in the world leading worthwhile lives who don't make "power lists" or other modern totems of transcendence. I knew a man who was so distraught at not having made the Forbes 400 list of the richest Americans that he sent a team of accountants to the publication to prove his bona fides. He eventually made it. This person had endured threats to his family *before* making the list but still hungered for more visibility.

I'm always skeptical when very successful people tell me they don't need recognition. The desire to be appreciated and to feel as if you've made your mark is a very human one. I expressed affectionate disbelief when a mogul friend who kept a very low profile told me that he longed only for anonymity.

"You don't believe me?" he asked.

"I believe that you have your ego under control," I said. "I don't believe you have no need for recognition. There's a difference."

Whatever inner need my friend had for recognition, the counterweights were the consequences of a high profile: investigations, kidnapping, burglaries, lawsuits, employee unrest, shakedowns, loss of privacy, sieges by salesmen, relatives, and charities asking for more, more, more. He knew all of this and made the decision to market his business but avoid the limelight personally, something that was accepted in his field. But I don't believe he simply lacked the interest in having his success acknowledged.

I have long been fascinated by Jacqueline Kennedy Onassis, one of the most famous people in the world during the second half of the twentieth century. She rose to prominence under extraordinary circumstances, the brief rise and violent fall of her husband, President John F. Kennedy. For the remainder of her life, she remained a subject of fascination because of these extraordinary circumstances, but also because, despite unrelenting Kennedy dramas, Onassis resisted the urge to work the press. She knew that in her unusual case, the best spin was no spin.

When everybody thinks they are a brand in a culture that believes it has a constitutional right to know everything about everybody, a collective misassumption emerges that we are required to provide the world with running commentary about our lives. In the midst of reputation-ending controversy, there are situations where a response is essential, but there is a capricious correlation between actions and effects. Onassis recognized the futility of trying to change prejudicial minds and refused to climb into the clown car of self-promoters who were the precursors to the Kardashian era. In the process, she became an icon.

In terms of raw survival, one of the best examples of leveraging a low profile to one's advantage is to contrast the reigns of organized crime bosses Vincent "the Chin" Gigante of the Genovese family and John Gotti of the Gambino clan. Authorities now believe that Gigante ruled the Genoveses from the early 1980s until his death in prison in 2005. He was a major force in that organization for decades prior. Gigante feigned mental illness by walking the streets of Greenwich Village in his bathrobe, muttering to himself. He insisted that other men become known as the boss in order to distract attention away from him. He had a strict rule that the very mention of his name out loud would result in a death sentence lest

New York Magazine

anyone be captured on tape talking about him. Any reference to him had to be made by touching one's chin, signifying his nickname.

John Gotti took a different approach. After shooting his way to the top by leaving his boss dead in a Manhattan gutter, Gotti spent his next five years as Don in one long self-coronation. This included a $30,000 per night gambling habit, holding court in popular restaurants, a *Time* magazine cover story with a portrait painted by Andy Warhol, and weekly meetings at his Little Italy social club, where he demanded his men pay homage.

So predictable—and public—was Gotti's behavior that the FBI was able to identify the Gambino leadership and eavesdrop on his meetings. Gotti discussed a variety of crimes, including murders, which led to his arrest and conviction.

Vincent Gigante New York Daily News Archive/Getty Images

While Gotti and Gigante both died in prison, Gigante's discretion and indirection kept him at the helm of his outfit for about a quarter century, as opposed to Gotti's few years. Moreover, Gotti presided over his gang's demise by throwing his lifestyle in the faces of law enforcement. Gigante, on the other hand, built his gang into what mob watchers have called the "Rolls-Royce" of organized crime from the shadows. It took the authorities decades to accurately realize his status.

The gangster life may be abhorrent, but on a jungle level, we can learn something from who rises, who implodes, and why, in a field with a high morbidity rate. Indeed, it happens at the highest orders of society, too: French finance minister Nicolas Fouquet, whose profile rose too high for the liking of Louis XIV, earned himself a trip to prison, where he died.

Even in the narcissism of the digital frontier, there are still people who want to be left alone. Publicity has benefits but also a price. Before pursuing it, consider how much you want to pay.

Kobayashi Maru

My preoccupation with the laws of my home planet never afforded me an appreciation of *Star Trek*, but there was one particular sequence that stayed with me. It is known in Trek-lore as Kobayashi Maru, which was a simulated test of character. In the simulation, young cadets got to play the role of captain of the starship *Enterprise*. Another starship, the *Kobayashi Maru*, sends a distress signal from a particularly lethal region in outer space. The *Enterprise* captain has two choices. One, she can attempt to rescue the *Kobayashi Maru*, but to do so would force them to violate enemy space and be annihilated. Two, she can let the troubled ship perish, and the *Enterprise* will survive.

The cadet "captains" often feel a sense of failure because they were unable to come up with a solution, mistakenly believing they had been presented with a solvable puzzle. They hadn't been—because there was no answer in the sense that a standardized test has an answer.

The point of Kobayashi Maru was to see how potential leaders responded to a no-win situation. Some cadets still approached the exercise as a puzzle, racking their brains for the right answer. Others whined that it was an unfair test. But the lesson was that in order to be a real leader, you needed to look at situations in all of their messiness, make decisions accordingly, and learn to redefine success when conventional command-and-control assessments are no longer workable.

There are very real consequences to the glass jaw syndrome, namely, an operating environment that places a premium on: risk-avoidance over thoughtful risk-taking; brittle templates over improvisation; gentle lies over difficult truths; saying the right thing over doing the right thing; and a belief in technologies that have benefits but even more risks.

Cultural climates and technologies change. There are many brilliant minds at work, which assures us only that tomorrow's communications will be different from today's. The same social media that now pose such a problem for the scandalized may hold unexpected promises in the future but not likely anytime soon. Said the *New York Times*'s Thomas Friedman, "Something really big happened in the world's wiring in the last decade, but it was obscured by the financial crisis and post-9/11. We went from a connected world to a hyper-connected world. I'm always struck that Facebook, Twitter, 4G, iPhones, iPads, ubiquitous wireless and Web-enabled cellphones, the cloud, Big Data, cellphone apps and Skype did not exist or were in their infancy a decade ago."

The velocity with which information travels will only increase. It is hard to imagine a countervailing technology that will alter the human thirst for information, true or false, or will facilitate deliberation. Technology and other forces have simply shifted us from a plane where we savage the unloved with bloody ball spikes to savaging them with the click of a mouse.

Reputations as Hostages

This book has been my attempt to convey the new dynamics of surviving controversies, not because I have all the answers, but because the first step in finding cures is nailing the pathologies. Just as watching a palooka's jaw get shattered decades ago by a seemingly lesser fighter opened my eyes to the realities of boxing, my experiences with the targets of public wrath over the past three decades have led me to revisit conventional—and my own— wisdom about crisis management.

The mission of this book has been to awaken readers to the changing nature of controversy with the hope that this will help you avoid and, if you must, survive it. As we contemplate solutions, there is no more dangerous mindset than *Well, they must know what they're doing.* . . . The "they" in this scenario are leaders and experts in whom we invest a lot of confidence without good reason.

If crisis managers can't attack the efficacy of our own business models, someone else will do it for us, and the results won't be pretty. Regardless, the current fetish of spin doctors and their reputational elixirs will be stripped bare as more decision makers recognize that much of what is being merchandized doesn't actually work. As we learned in *The Wizard of Oz*, the great and powerful wizard is just a little guy from Kansas hiding behind some drapes.

All revolutions have casualties, and we are at the beginning of one. If I were not hopeful about the capacity of scandal principals to emerge from controversies, it wouldn't be worth writing books or running a business rooted in the premise that it is done all the time. Nevertheless, it isn't done by mesmerists or, as Michael Clayton suggested, by janitors. I would compare my career to a different specialty: hostage negotiation. A malcontented party already has a hostage, my client's reputation, and is holding a dead man's switch so every potential rescue maneuver has serious consequences.

The key is to get through scandal with minimal losses. To do so requires an understanding of human psychology, imagination, improvisation, realism, resources, and the kinds of tactics that do and don't apply to these scenarios. *After all, we don't really "manage" crises as much as we do negotiate them with kidnappers. Management* implies control; *negotiation* acknowledges other forces at work.

Many scandal-plagued people and institutions survive and prosper. Realism is the main ingredient in a survival cocktail. Getting knocked down can be healthy, provided that the experience frightens but doesn't destroy. Inexperience with mortal terror leads to a false sense of invincibility, specifically a feeling that your good fortune is a function of superior management of one's affairs. There are two kinds of confidence in life: the confidence of having been decked and returned to your feet, and the confidence that comes with never having been hit and misattributing it to prowess.

Samuel Johnson said, "When a man knows he is to be hanged in a fortnight, it concentrates his mind wonderfully." The same is true about surviving a controversy where you learn the ways of the universe quickly and with great clarity.

Those facing and negotiating crisis and scandal should disenthrall themselves with the power of communications. As Adam Gopnik wrote of Winston Churchill in the *New Yorker*, "Churchill's words did all that words can do in the world. They said what had to be done; they announced why it had to be done; they inspired those who had to do it." There came a point, though, when Churchill and the Allies needed an army, tanks, and guns. We must look for redemption in the form of excellence in products produced, services rendered, skills practiced, policies pursued, and good works accomplished.

Despite my cynicism about the fictional spin doctors of show business, there is a conjurer I have admired since I first saw him in action and who offers wisdom for today's challenges. I am referring to the healer, Miracle Max (Billy Crystal), in the 1986 film *The Princess Bride*. He's world-weary and skeptical, but his heart is good. Max is a master of making the best of bad situations, and he assures his desperate clients that their mortally wounded friend, the hero Westley, is merely "mostly dead."

By reframing Westley's recovery as one that would emphasize endurance over escape in addition to his magic potion, Miracle Max returns Westley to his former swashbuckling self. As Max admonishes, "Don't rush me, sonny. You rush a miracle man, you get rotten miracles."

Acknowledgments

I would like to thank the following people for their support and direction in the writing of *Glass Jaw*:

My editor, Sean Desmond, and Libby Burton of Twelve books; Kris Dahl of ICM; my family, Donna, Stuart, and Eliza; Danika Robinson, who provided research support; my colleagues at Dezenhall Resources Ltd., James Hewitt, Aaron Saunders, Nicki Neily, Maya Shackley, Steven Schlein, Josh Culling, Anne Marie Malecha, Cathy Brasfield, and Jennifer Hirshon; Bill Novelli, Cathy Tinsley, and Robin Dillon-Merrill of the McDonough School of Business; and Sarah Rosenzweig, my teaching assistant at McDonough.

I would also like to thank Bob Stein, Walt Buchholtz, Paul Fox, Jimmy Lynn, Cary Bernstein, Norman Ornstein, Sally Satel, Tom Clare, Libby Locke, and Jordan Lieberman.

Index

Note: Page numbers in *italics* refer to illustrations.